GRUMPY OLD MEN

GRUMPY OLD MEN
STUART PREBBLE

B B C
BOOKS

This book is published to accompany the television series entitled *Grumpy Old Men,* which was first broadcast in October 2003 (first series) and September 2004 (second series). The series was produced by Liberty Bell Productions for BBC Television.
Executive producer: Stuart Prebble
Producer/Director: Alan Lewens

Published by BBC Books,
BBC Worldwide Ltd, Woodlands,
80 Wood Lane, London W12 0TT

First published 2004
Reprinted 2004 (three times)

ISBN 0 563 52209 7

Commissioning editors: Benn Dunn and Shirley Patton
Project editor: Rachel Copus
Copy editor: Trish Burgess
Illustrator: Martin Shovel
Designer: Annette Peppis
Production controller: Christopher Tinker

Set in Stone serif and Erazure

Printed and bound in Great Britain by CPI Bath

For more information about this and other BBC books, please visit our website on www.bbcshop.com or telephone 08700 777001.

Contents

Foreword

ARTHUR SMITH

New Year's Eve 2003. It is raining heavily and I am just arriving at the Angel underground station when a teenage girl spots me. 'Look at him!' she cries to no one I can see, 'The Grumpy Old Man!' Suddenly from out of the darkness a dozen more girls appear screaming excitedly, surround me and my girlfriend and point. I am proclaimed 'The Coolest Man in London'. It has been a long, dry road but finally, as I am about to hit 50, I have been mobbed by schoolgirls. How can this be? What have I done to merit this marvellous attention?

The story starts six months earlier when I am asked to appear on a new TV programme. You'll know the kind of show – they've been a TV staple for a couple of years now; a bunch of people you can't quite place say stuff that's not that perceptive about something you're not especially interested in. Cut around the talking heads are bits of old footage related to the subject – usually a perky exercise in nostalgia along the lines of 'I love 1990' or 'Beckham: The Early Years'. Like most television, it is neither very good nor very bad. Blandly undemanding, it exists in order that there be no gap in the channel's output, no pause in the relentless chattering of the box. The 'celebrities' who pop up on them usually talk and think in tabloid headlines and are identifiable by an air of smugness. I have been on five such programmes.

This latest one I had agreed to do was intriguing. *Grumpy Old Men* is a more abstract concept than *The Top Ten Ugliest People in Britain* or *Celebrating Dad's Army*. And why had they asked me? I'm middle-aged rather than old and I'm no more grumpy than the next man. But as I slouched along the street thinking about it, I realised that the next man is extremely grumpy and that I only have to look at the typical Nike-infested teenager with his iPod and his 'attitude' to feel very old indeed.

So it was I found myself outside a pub near Oxford Circus one afternoon in early summer being teed up by the director to whinge about a range of subjects covering most facets of modern life. I started slowly, stammering, like a nervous customer trying to get a refund, but as I went on I gathered momentum. Slowly a surge of indignation began to swell forth from deep in my bowels and I soon found myself complaining freely and with joyous vigour about the distressing business of being alive and middle-aged at the start of the third millennium.

So many times in trains, in shops or banks, on the phone, all over the place I had bitten my tongue to avoid shouting at idiotic bureaucrats, snapping at moronic juveniles or threatening people in queues, and here, now, I was invited, paid even, to verbalise every cantankerous thought I had ever had about the world. Life is shit organised by bastards. Everywhere you look things are faulty. The train is late, your sandwich is all PR and no filling, politics are spinning out of control, we're obsessed with trivia and our souls are drowning in corporate consumerism. Meanwhile, the whole world is conspiring to make your life more difficult, every jumped-up paperboy with a clipboard or a uniform is tinkering away trying to sabotage the workings of the Grumpy Old Man and keep him from his chosen pastime of sitting around in his underpants. As I railed on and on, I became increasingly energised and excited by my own misery and misanthropy until I reached a kind of orgasm of negativity.

Afterwards I had a cigarette, calmed down and forgot about the whole thing. I returned to grumbling silently or only in the company of close friends, fellow Grumpy Old Men who would counter my disapproval of modern footballers with their own polemics about IKEA or computers or dentists. I thought *Grumpy Old Men* was going to be only one programme that would go out late, make very little impression and be quietly forgotten – as has occurred in the great majority of my previous appearances on TV.

But I was wrong. Stuart had eked out the material into a four-part series, got a plum spot and a surprisingly large dollop of pre-publicity. My fellow grumpies were, disappointingly, extremely funny. Ken Stott and Rick Stein seemed bludgeoned into disbelief at the inanities of our times, Matthew Parris refused to know who Catherine Zeta Jones is, John Peel blinked despairingly, Bob Geldof was vitriolic and foul-mouthed, Bill Nighy, then a little-known ballet dancer, announced he had no plans for penile extension. There was an assault on the burgeoning misuse of the apostrophe by Tony Hawks, who had once written to Ken Livingstone to ask why Earl's Court had one but Barons Court didn't. Ken's reply was apparently shot through with apostrophic errors, which Tony generously chose to believe were deliberate.

My own favourite contributor was the cadaverous Will Self who worked himself up into high and eloquent dudgeon. This was his ad-libbed take on mobile phones: 'What they promote is a meaningless level of anonymous chit-chat with people, where you don't actually have to get down and dirty and smell somebody or see their body language. They're actually the very key representation of the anomie and alienation of our culture. … And when it comes down – when it all falls down about us – all that will be left in the wreckage of our civilisation is a single tiny little black oblong going, "diddle dee dah, diddle dee dah, diddle dee dah," and there'll be nobody to answer it.' In a way the series was a televisual version of stand-up comedy – a form that thrives on slagging things off. Any comic will tell you it's very hard to be funny and nice at the same time.

These talking heads were glued together by Stuart's bile, a potent brew that had obviously been fermenting for longer than was good for him. A stream of images illustrated the grim script, which was delivered with masterful dry disdain by Geoffrey Palmer. This book reprises Stuart's gripes and adds more, for truly he is a prolifically miserable git. Impressively, he has also managed to cobble up a theory explaining just how deeply emblematic and significant the Grumpy Old Man is and how, after living through the 1960s, he is more disappointed than any previous generation of Grumpies.

Before the first series went out I expected any critical attention it drew would be unfavourable. Who, after all, would enjoy old blokes peeving? And no one wants ugly people clogging up airtime. 'Pack it in, Grandad, and get back to your shed.' Yet critics liked the programme, and more than one lamented loudly that he had not participated. Stuart told me he thought some reviews were written as audition pieces for the second series.

A chord was struck with the public too; not just with all the other Grumpy Old Men in the country, but with their wives, children, friends and lovers too. If I didn't hate the word 'Zeitgeist', I'd use it in a sentence now. I lost count of the number of times I was stopped and told, 'I know someone just like you.' Well, no, in fact, I didn't lose count. It happened six times. It was a bit annoying. I didn't mind so much, though, when young women confided that they too suffered the same frustrations we were complaining about. You don't have to be old or male to have an inner grouch longing to get out. For example, no human being of any stripe could fail to be infuriated when caught up in some complex 'press-star-to-hear-these-options-again' telephonic nightmare. We all sometimes feel like Peter Finch in *Network*: 'I'm mad as hell and I'm not going to take it any more!' We TV Grumpies were giving public voice to the secret carpings of the nation.

So well done, Stuart, for identifying a trend, for finally providing me with the pathetic pleasure of feeling like a teenies' pop idol and now for milking the whole thing once more to create this book. And if by chance you're reading this 50 years after it was written, perhaps leafing through it in the back of a second-hand book shop, you'll wonder what it was all about and who we all were. But probably not for very long. Put the book back and leave us grumbling and whingeing in the eternal disappointment of our graves.

And a Merry Christmas to you, Vicar!

Introduction

Do you remember all those programmes presented by Clive James in which he showed clips of television shows from around the world? We'd all chortle superciliously at the plywood sets, the plastic actors and the brittle dialogue from awful soaps made in far-off lands occupied by funny people whose names were Gerda or Tammy or Kenji. It provided us with harmless fun, reinforced our sense of superiority, and made us even more grateful than we already were to be in the land that invented *It Ain't Half Hot Mum*.

Clive used to reserve the sharpest bits of his special brand of wit for the programmes made by the Japanese. He would show us what that apparently very odd nation called entertainment, which involved taking real people, or sometimes people whom we were told were B-list celebrities, and putting them through all sorts of torture. Maybe they would have to insert their heads into a bucket of maggots and come out with a plastic key in their mouths, or perhaps they would have to wade through animal dung filled with eels to grab some trinket. Do you remember? Contestants would have to drink gallons of water and not take a piss, while over-excited TV hosts emptied watering cans slowly in front of them.

My, how we laughed. Clive would deliver ever more tortured similes through his adenoids, and we would cringe and watch the screen from between our fingers. We were not, of course, laughing at the programmes; no, no, there was little about them that was even remotely amusing for a nation as sophisticated as ours. We were laughing at the Japanese. Didn't it just tell you everything you needed to know about these strange and horrid little people that this was what they regarded as peak-time entertainment? These were the guys we'd seen featured in *Bridge on the River Kwai* and *Tenko*. We'd read about them in comic books as being those awful, slanty-eyed little chaps with peaked caps who yelled 'Banzai' a lot, before further brutalising one of our brave Tommies. Is it any wonder that they got off on seeing people tortured and humiliated? Weird little buggers. Thank God it's them and not us.

I think maybe we can abbreviate the rest of this because, short of reaching for an oversized builder's trowel and laying it on even thicker, I suspect you can see where this is heading. It was into the TV environment that had recently spawned *I'm a Celebrity, Get Me out of Here* that I returned to resume my career as a programme-maker after half a dozen years of being what TV people refer to as 'a suit'. Although I had held a lot of jobs running programme departments and commissioning ideas from others, my last real 'hands-on' job making programmes myself had been as a producer of *World in Action* – a magnificent dinosaur of a current affairs series, which had become extinct on ITV years ago.

So how to re-establish myself in a world that had moved so far and so fast since I'd been away? The first thing I realised was that I needed to start with something on which I felt really expert.

Oh yes, I found it all right.

To be honest, when I first dreamt up the idea of making a

TV series called *Grumpy Old Men* I had a sneaking concern that it might just be me – or that perhaps it was just me and a few friends. Maybe there were only a few of us who went about our everyday business, seeming to the outside world to be reasonably well-balanced and affable, but all the time secretly plagued by a continuous running commentary going on our heads. 'When did it become all right to advertise a telephone enquiry line and then not employ anyone to answer the phone?' Or 'When did it become OK to put half an hour of bilious nonsense on the cinema screen at the time they've advertised as the start-time of the film?' Or, even more mundanely, 'What on earth does he think he looks like?'

Was it just a few of us who were mentally parsing the grammar of every announcement on the train or railway station? Or gently shaking our heads or sucking our teeth at every greengrocer's apostrophe? Or cursing under our breath every time there was a new sleeping policeman further trying to obstruct our already damn nearly impossible drive to work?

The BBC had told producers that it wanted to develop ideas for TV series that said something new about 'the way we live now' (and that's another thing – people who put inverted commas around everything whether it's justified or not). Well, I thought, maybe it's bonkers, but I can honestly say that this idea is authentically about the way I live now.

Like every independent TV producer worth his salt, I did thorough and comprehensive research. I asked my mate Andrew McLaughlin, who is about the same age as I am and shares a similar sort of mindset, if he recognised the phenomenon I was describing. He didn't need to have it explained to him for more than two minutes, and I knew that he'd got it in one because over the next few days after the conversation I started receiving a stream of emails entitled 'And another thing'. These included rants about restaurants that add a 10 per cent service charge to the bill, and then leave a blank space where the total should be so you might not notice and add another 10 per cent. Menus that say 'pan-fried' or 'oven-baked': how else can you fry something than in a pan? Might as well say 'grill-grilled'.

Eventually I wrote it up, in about three pages, and sent it to the BBC. Jane Root, the controller of BBC2, got it straight away – she told me that she recognised the 'Grumpy Old Man' phenomenon instantly because she occasionally lives with one. Inevitably, I found myself thinking, does she occasionally live with a Grumpy Old Man, and sometimes with someone else, or is the man she lives with occasionally grumpy? (Turns out to be the last and she has recently married him – so we must be doing something right.)

The commissioning editor Jo Clinton-Davis told me that she had laughed out loud as she walked down the corridor reading it – surely a good sign – but was not quite certain if the idea would extend to a series. I would have to write up some more.

I took my laptop computer away with me on holiday – to the Maldives as a matter of fact – and got up early every morning – 4 o'clock actually – and started tapping away. And if you are a female reader, I already know what you're thinking – what about this bastard's poor wife? I know, I know, and there's a chapter later on that goes into some of her advice on how to survive living with a grumpy old git. Turns out that grumpies' wives need to be more than averagely affable – but stop: already we're getting ahead of ourselves.

Now it's not easy to be grumpy in the Maldives; it is as close as you can get to paradise and still be on the planet – but grumpiness is not about the immediate environment. Indeed, it follows you everywhere you go, literally to the ends of the Earth. Certainly I was grumpy about all the Chinese people who had suddenly started coming to the resort and whose idea of

personal space wasn't the same as mine, and who seemed to
think it was OK to clear their throats noisily at breakfast. And I
do mean 'clear'. I was grumpy that the wooden hut we stayed in
was 50 yards further up the beach than the last time we had
visited, and that the decor had been changed to the mock-
Polynesian favoured by certain airports. I was grumpy about
VHS milk or whatever it's called in those little cartons you get
on aeroplanes and that always spill all over you when you try to
open them. But these were just the immediate grumps: not far
behind them was the queue of stuff that has irritated me day in,
day out for years and years. And it grows. Every day. Alarmingly.

Next time I looked, three pages had become 27 pages, and I
was still writing. Better stop, I thought – we may be creating a
monster we can't control. When I got home I sent the updated
proposal to the BBC. I'm not sure what the 27 pages did for Jo
Clinton-Davis – she started looking at me a bit strangely after
that, and would occasionally enquire solicitously about my
wife and family. Anyhow, it sure as hell was cathartic for me. In
any event, it convinced everyone who needed convincing that
this idea had legs. There was certainly enough material to
produce a series. More than enough. Once I get started on
aspects of the world we have created that drive me nuts, I could
go on...and on...and on... And I do.

So we had a series to make, and next I needed to find the
right person to direct it. I'll come straight to the point: I think I
found the only person in the whole of British broadcasting who
is grumpier than I am. If you wonder if this is possible, try
phoning Alan Lewens on his mobile and listen to the message.
It sounds exactly as it would if it were the seventieth time
you've phoned him today and he was asking, 'What on earth
could you possibly want now?' It more or less defies you to
leave a message, and that is undoubtedly the intention. Alan
made clear that he didn't really know what he was letting

himself in for, but work is work and a BBC2 series is a BBC2 series, so let's hope that someone aboard this project knows what the hell it is we are talking about.

Not only is Alan a little grumpier than me, he is also a little older than me, and he felt strongly that we would need someone younger and of the opposite gender to balance our combined weight – by which I mean gravitas rather than bulk, though that too. He found Jackie Baker, a talented and delightful associate producer, who was also not sure what on earth she had let herself in for but was obviously game. Jackie turned out to be marvellous, but I did worry a bit about her when we started trying to cast the series.

She said that we wouldn't be able to tell people what the series was called, or no one would agree to participate. Who would willingly class themselves as anything so unendearing as a Grumpy Old Man? This was to miss the point alarmingly. I responded that if people were not happy to identify themselves under this heading, then they very definitely were not what we were looking for. Grumpy Old Men know exactly who they are, and are not at all reluctant to admit that they are one. If I was wrong and we couldn't cast the series on this basis, then the whole idea wouldn't work. And having secured the commission from the BBC on the basis that it would, believe me, we were going to make it work.

Well, we were both right. We were turned down by all sorts of people whom you might expect to jump at the sobriquet, but we got an instant sense of recognition from the genuine article. Arthur Smith didn't need to be asked twice: he is the embodiment of Grumpy Old Man, noticing and commenting on the absurdities of just about everything we see around us is what he does for a living. Thus art perfectly imitates life. Will Self also exemplifies the phenomenon: sickened to the stomach by all the crap you see everywhere you look, but expressing his insights in such deliciously colourful metaphors. If I'd just had the foresight to recognise it, I think Rick Wakeman would probably have paid me for the chance to participate. In the event, he bought me lunch and told me he'd go anywhere at any time to be interviewed. And he then thanked me several times for asking. Very nice man is Rick.

Bob Geldof didn't need any persuading that he was a Grumpy Old Man – who, indeed, could doubt it? The only problem was that he was too grumpy to be bothered to participate. In the end he agreed as a personal favour, and then enjoyed himself so much that he persuaded Michael Grade to come on board. It turned out later that Michael was doing it in a craven attempt to improve his chances of being appointed Chairman of the BBC, but we didn't know that at the time. Much as Bill Nighy used it as a springboard to get the part in *Love Actually*. We made these people what they are today, but do they thank us? Well, that's another story. Rory McGrath, John O'Farrell, Rick Stein, John Peel, Bill Nighy, Lemn Sissay, Felix Dexter – they all recognised the phenomenon straight away.

The best part was that they didn't really know exactly what it was we wanted from them. Usually you can explain a programme idea by saying, 'It's a bit like *They Think It's All Over* or a bit like *Wife Swap*.' Then they can give you the interview they think you want. *Grumpy Old Men* wasn't really a bit like anything. 'What?' said Tony Hawks, in a comment that eventually provided the finale to the series, 'You get a group of boring oldish gits and get them to ramble on about everything that gets on their nerves? And you expect people to sit at home and watch it?' Yep, that was about the size of it.

So we got started. Positively seeking out all the sources of irritation we would usually try so hard to avoid. Going out and filming in multistorey car parks, where the slopes are so close together you have to do a three-point turn to go from one to the next and then the bays are too small to park an electric toaster. Joining the marauding hordes at IKEA on a Saturday, and having people puzzle for hours and days on end over self-assembly furniture. Or hanging on for 40 minutes to try to get through to the British Airways call centre and listening to canned Vivaldi until you want to thrust your fist down the receiver, grab someone by the throat and drag them back into your living room for ritual dismemberment.

After several weeks of this, it's fair to say there were times when Alan and I wondered if we had lost the plot. Or, indeed, if there had ever been a plot to lose. Alan is a veteran producer and director, with a distinguished career involving classy documentaries about everything from Frank Sinatra's voice to Stephen Fry and Paddington Bear. I can still recall the look on his face when I told him that I wanted to find a sign attached to a lamppost that said 'MASSIVE RUG SALE' so that we could wonder out loud about how many people would want to buy a massive rug. Or occasionally I'd go off on one about all the white lines and red lines and yellow lines and chevrons and studs and railings and cycle lanes and assorted road signs that have completely vandalised the route out of Salisbury going to Southampton, and I could see him mentally waving goodbye to his career.

Well, turns out we needn't have worried. I got the first inkling that we had tapped into something when we sent over the opening sequence of programme one to be included in the BBC tape that would launch the autumn season to the press. It consisted of a series of one-liners from our Grumpy Old Men: 'The instant you walk out of your front door, you see something that annoys you' (Arthur Smith). 'School plays are universally and uniformly shite' (Bob Geldof). 'Death penalty, it has to be public and it has to be a beheading – men over 30 with ponytails' (John Sessions). 'I hate the phrase "traffic-calming"' (Richard Madeley). 'Turn the fucking music down' (Rory McGrath). At the launch event several instalments were drowned out by the laughter. And it wasn't just what they said, it was the way they said it. With a passion and sincerity that came from the heart. It seemed that every time we pressed a hot button, they 'went off on one'. You can only imagine my relief to discover that I was not alone – far from it.

The reaction to the series was such an overwhelming 'Hear, hear' that I think we've created a movement. Not a political party, because Grumpy Old Men are united much more by what we are against than by what we are in favour of (though on reflection that may make us more cohesive than New Labour). No, it's not so much a TV series but more a way of life. As Bob Geldof put it, 'If you aren't grumpy, it means that you are content with the world around you, and who the fuck in their right mind would be that?'

CHAPTER 1

Identifying Grumpy Old Men

So who exactly are we?

Now before we go very far down this path, we need to make one thing very clear. It's a sort of a health warning, and it's this. Ready? There is absolutely no scientific or intellectual rigour underpinning anything to do with *Grumpy Old Men*. Everything in it is made up. There are odd facts here and there, but these are by the by; most of what follows is entirely subjective. The fact that I am so irritated by John McCririck that I want to pop him in the liquidiser is just my personal perspective. For all I know, John may be a delightful bloke, good company, kind to animals and children. Nothing about it is objective or scientific: he just gets on my wick.

It seems necessary to mention this because one particularly clever fellow said to us after the first series went out that it was a bit odd that we had talked so much about growing up in the '60s, and then included interviews with people such as Rory McGrath, who was clearly too young to have known much about that decade. Alan briefly and valiantly tried to defend the thesis by explaining that the '60s were a phenomenon that affected everyone, whether you'd lived through them or not. I had to stop him short.

'Don't even go there,' I said. 'You must understand that nothing in this proposition has any basis in reality. We can't really argue anything in it beyond the level of assertion.' Which is what I'm accused of all the time anyway. 'Let's think for a moment how best to characterise this. Oh yes, I have it. It's all bollocks.'

The discussion got better after that, and it's as well to know from the start that the same applies to the book as applied to the series. There will hardly be a statement in it that we can prove or that, if challenged, we could be bothered even to argue about. If you find yourself disagreeing with any of the various vile and unjust prejudices ahead, take comfort from the fact that you are almost certainly right, and we are almost certainly wrong. Better than that, it also probably means that you are a much nicer person than we are – though of course this may also put you into the group that Grumpy Old Men would refer to as 'a bit of a prat'. There you are, already an unjust and uncalled-for bit of prejudice.

Also, if you are one of those 'that can't be true because he can only have been about five years old in 1963' people, I'd be inclined to see if you have still got the receipt from the bookshop, or close the book before you've bent the spine any more and give it away as a present to any unmitigated grumpy of your acquaintance. My guess is that this might include just about any man who knows you. Are you with me?

So back to the only thing that has been scientifically proven, which came my way in autumn 2002. I was sitting at the desk in the only room in my house where I try to do any serious thinking – the office – reading the *Daily Telegraph* with a nice cup of tea and a couple of ginger snaps, as you do, when I caught sight of an article that said, 'Middle-aged men are the new grumps.' Or something like that anyway. Being of the middle-aged persuasion myself, I extended my arms to their utmost extent but still could not find the right focal length. I scrabbled about among the landfill of unpaid bills, tax demands and unsolicited mail from estate agents on my desk, still failed to find my specs, and so squinted at the irritatingly small type, grumbling quietly to myself as I did so.

It was a report of a survey that found men aged 35–54 were the grumpiest of any in history. This group, according to the survey, contained those least likely to believe that 'our leaders know better than we do'. Yeah, right. 'That the NHS is getting better.' On what planet might that be? 'That technology is improving our lives.' Oh yes, like 'Press 1 for balance details, 2 for mortgage enquiries, 3 for pizza and 4 for an outsize strippagram.'

Now I know that, with the advent of 24-hour news channels on TV and radio, daily newspapers no longer think it worthwhile to carry news, but this seemed to me to be an unusually blinding glimpse of the obvious. Who on earth could possibly imagine that things are getting better? You would have to be deaf, dumb and blind. Well, on reflection, Helen Keller might think things are getting better, but even then only if she had just in the last few minutes reached the front of the 12-year waiting list for a seeing and hearing dog.

So since it must be manifestly obvious to anyone that the world is going to hell in a hand-basket, I began to wonder why it was that this appreciation appeared to be concentrated among people of about my age. You would sort of expect the grumpiest people in the community to be the oldest, shuffling around the place, dribbling and incontinent and muttering, 'Things ain't what they used to be.' This was the group we all felt most sorry for when we were growing up. The group apparently most alienated from what we laughingly call the 'mainstream' today.

However, it turns out that the older generation is relatively content. They are happy to have survived the war and lived to tell the tale, often endlessly. And so crap was their youth, growing up with rationing and then being told, 'You've never had it so good' by aristocratic arse-heads, that their expectations were low. They didn't think that things would get a whole hell of a lot better, and, blow me, they didn't. But for many of them they didn't get a lot worse either. Most of them have worked all their lives and are now enjoying a pension – which some of them even started receiving index-linked just before that particular joy became a distant and fast-receding memory.

Obviously nobody expected younger groups to be grumpy. You might expect them to be dissatisfied with the state of the world (and the fact that they are not turns out to be one of the major reasons why my age group is grumpy). Anyhow, it seems that collectively they don't really think enough about the world outside them to be grumpy about it. 'They are concerned about their world,' as Richard Madeley succinctly put it, 'not about the world.'

So, 35–54-year-olds. The grumpiest of any demographic group. Well, that felt about right to me. At the time of reading the article I was 51, and of course I knew that I was grumpy – I've dined out on it for years – but it did come as a surprise to read that so many of my contemporaries were too.

I asked a few of my mates. Obviously we all have the same general irritations – teenage kids, people using their mobiles on trains, body piercing, that sort of thing, but did they feel generally grumpy about the state of the world around them? A sense that it was irritating not just here and there, but just about every bloody where? I found that quite a few of them recognised the syndrome. So I started wondering why we, in many ways maybe the luckiest of any generation in history, should feel this way, and what we have in common.

At the root of the point here is that mostly we are children of the '50s, whose views and outlook were formed in the '60s and '70s, and who grew up thinking the world would be a better place, but found that in most ways it isn't.

Those were the days when our idea of a cool gadget was a little knife in the shape of a tube for taking the core out of an apple, or five parallel blades embedded in a square of plastic to speed up slicing runner beans. We got a kick out of the implement on the side of a penknife designed to take a stone out of a horse's hoof: and since we lived on a council estate in West Norwood and the only horse we ever saw belonged to the rag-and-bone man, there wasn't a lot of call for it. Our idea of a thrill was to look at our friends through the coloured cellophane wrapped around our Easter egg. We sat in gloomy classrooms in the days when the world was still in black and white, and watched scratchy films showing us what life would be like in the future. In these films happy families would arrive at the breakfast bar perfectly groomed and rested, and sit with other members of the perfect family while robotic devices would offer a range of coloured pills and energy drinks. No beef dripping on white toast for them.

In these households there were no dishes to wash and no ironing to do. After a moment or two of inconsequential conversation, you would wave goodbye to your Stepford family and step forth through a sliding door that saw you coming and whisked back noiselessly. Then you would enter a sleek glass bullet hovering a few inches above a monorail on which other happy families were also gliding smoothly, waving to each other, with no fear that anyone would come close enough for anything more intimate than the exchange of an inane smile. No steering wheels, no brakes, no traffic jams, just the patronising voice of a woman telling you your diary for the day. 'Manicure at 11. Meeting Miss Kilobyte at one. Intergalactic conference call at three.'

You'd be dropped off at work, a stainless-steel office, where all the women wore figure-hugging mini-dresses, sported Helen Shapiro hairstyles, and had a look on their faces that suggested they would shag you any time you wanted. Or maybe that was more a function of my febrile mind than anything actually in

the film, but in my defence I should say that all my mates at
school claimed to have caught that same glint.

Since computers had taken all the nasty hard part out of
thinking, you'd fiddle about for a little while, making sure all of
Earth's support systems were whirring away nicely, and then go
home to be walked by the canine robot, and help the kids with
their history homework, which would be about the bleak and
grey old days of the '50s and '60s before we could control the
weather and Liverpool still had a decent football team. (Of
course I'm making up that last bit – history would be unable to
recall the last time that Liverpool had a decent football team –
but you get the drift.)

We were young but we weren't stupid. Well, perhaps a bit
stupid if we thought the look on those girls' faces meant 'You
can shag me now', but even if you had asked us then, I don't
think we would have said we believed that we'd be going to
work on hovercrafts. On the other hand, we also didn't think
that we would be going to work in the same railway carriage –
yes, I mean *exactly* the same railway carriage – as the one we
were currently going to school in.

We didn't think we'd be so far away from our fellow
commuters that we'd scarcely be able to see their vacant and
sedative-induced smiles as they whisked past: on the other
hand, we probably also didn't think we would travel so
intimately alongside them on the Underground that we would
have no alternative but to savour the lingering odour of last
night's chicken madras. You can't open the newspapers without
reading about secondary smoking, but you don't see much
about secondary vindaloo, do you?

We probably didn't think our diet was going to consist of
perfectly balanced little coloured pills and vitamin drinks, but
we probably also didn't realise that we'd be eating so much
bloody rubbish that 20 per cent of men are obese, and in ten

years it will be 30 per cent. We probably also didn't anticipate salmonella in eggs, cholesterol and bacteria in milk, mad cow disease in beef or a deadly flu virus in chickens.

And when we heard the term 'convenience foods' we just thought we'd be peeling fewer potatoes and shelling fewer peas. It didn't occur to us then that the 'inconvenient food' that had been our lot for ever meant that the family had to be on hand to eat when the food was ready, rather than the other way around. Which meant in turn that the family had to get together in the same place at the same time, and might probably therefore be inclined to have a discussion. If someone had said at the time that 'convenience food' would mean that the food was on hand whenever you wanted it, and therefore that a staggering proportion of kids would be turning up at their first day at school unable to hold even a conversation because they have never, literally never, sat down to a family meal, we might not have embraced those revolutionary 'TV dinners' quite so warmly.

And so it goes on. We didn't anticipate global warming. We didn't anticipate weapons of mass destruction. We didn't anticipate Rupert Murdoch, and we didn't anticipate *I'm a Celebrity, Get Me out of Here*.

So, there we were: grey little kids, sneezing into grey little hankies, living in grey little houses, going to grey little classrooms, listening to grey little teachers talk about the yellow-brick road to a future in glorious Technicolor. Then, just as our characters were in the process of being formed by the rules of post-war rationing, conscription and Harold Macmillan, along came the Beatles, and all the rules went up in smoke.

It was great.

Most of us in this age group can remember where we were when we heard that Kennedy had been shot, and I reckon that most of us can remember where we were when we first heard the Beatles. I'm not sure if I was more attracted by the loud and sweaty music, or the fact that my parents reacted as though they were the Four Horsemen of the Apocalypse. Either way, it was the end of 'short back and sides' down at Ron's in Norwood High Street, and the beginning of a ten-year-long dispute with my mum and dad about the fact that I looked more like a girl than anything else.

I'm not going to go into this in detail because if you were there, you remember it, and if you weren't, you're bored stupid by it because other people have written about it far better than I could. Ad nauseam. However, suffice it to say that the promise of a technological future, coupled with the music and cultural revolution of the '60s, produced a generation that thought the world was going to get a lot better.

We sang, 'If you're going to San Francisco, be sure to wear some flowers in your hair.' Not many of us got to San Francisco, but quite a few of us got to Ibiza, or, failing that, the Isle of Wight, or, failing that, St Ives, or, failing that, the Hyde Park concerts – where Mick Jagger read some Shelley in memory of Brian Jones, danced in a white frock, and released a box of butterflies.

We rioted in Grosvenor Square, joined the march to Aldermaston and grew our hair to half-way down our backs to hack off our parents. We bought posters showing Che Guevara in black and white or the Beatles in psychedelic colours. We listened to Ummagumma, lit joss-sticks and, yes, we smoked a little bit of dope. We went to see *Easy Rider* at the cinema, made peace signs and said things such as 'far out', although we didn't really know what it meant, but it sure as hell felt good. We studied English or philosophy, or fine art or classics, and no one cared tuppence (that's two old pence) what grade of degree they would get so long as they passed it, and very few gave any thought to what they would do when they left. And we had quite a lot of casual sex too. Yes, kids – sorry – we invented it, not you. Though in fairness to you, for the most part we only used to do it in twos.

We were the first generation that wasn't going to go to war. The first generation to benefit from the welfare state. The first for whom spiritual things would be as important as material things.

So what happened next?

We elected Mrs Thatcher.

Who would have thought it? The kids who sang 'Ain't going to work on Maggie's farm no more' went off and elected her. And it's difficult to remember now how that felt, because one minute it was just a bit of a joke that this completely daft and dreadful old baggage had suddenly become the leader of the Tory party and was going around the place patronising everyone, and the next minute she was the bloody prime minister. It was one of those 'say it ain't so' moments.

In that one event many of the things our generation had hoped for started going out of the window. If it wasn't bad enough that she patronised everyone she met here, she insisted on going round the world patronising foreigners as well. As John Peel put it recently, 'You felt embarrassed to be British' and you wanted to write to the prime ministers of all the countries she had visited to apologise.

Anyway, I don't want to go too far into the politics of it all because a) it's very dull, b) a lot has already been written about it, and c) you probably don't agree with me anyway. Indeed, one of the worst things about it all was occasionally hearing people you quite liked saying, 'Well, it's about time someone sorted out the unions,' and having to choose between a quiet life and a fist-fight.

We all joined in when John and Yoko sang, 'All we are saying is give peace a chance,' and – guess what? – we went to the Falklands, to Bosnia, to Northern Ireland and to Iraq, twice. We sang, 'All you need is love' and went on to show that all you needed was love, a new car, a mortgage, a pension, enough money to fund the kids' education, private medical insurance and two foreign holidays a year.

So I guess that we're the guys who sang, 'Hope I die before I get old' and then, rather inconveniently, we didn't. We did get old and are still around.

CHAPTER 2

So how do you recognise one?

Although the core group of Grumpy Old Men is aged between 35 and 54, the phenomenon is far more widely shared than that. Indeed, the comment I've heard more often than any other since the TV series is, 'I'm one, and I'm not yet 35.' Or 'I'm one and I'm 58.' And these comments come just as often from women as they do from men.

There is no need to be concerned.

Grumpy Old Men can of course be under 35.

Grumpy Old Men can easily be over 54.

And while I am sure there are whole aircraft hangars full of stuff that irritates men but doesn't irritate women and vice versa, still there are strong areas of overlap.

So don't feel excluded just because you aren't a 35–54-year-old male. No sirree. The church of the Grumpy Old Men is a broad church. We welcome sinners and, unlike most churches, we don't invite you to repent. Grumpiness is not, of course, an age, nor is it a sex. It's simply a way of looking at the world.

And the best way to understand it is through what I call the 'AGA syndrome'.

Now before we get into details, this AGA syndrome stuff

sounds suspiciously like one of those pompous and ridiculous post-rationalisations that has been imposed on a perfectly obvious and straightforward phenomenon to make the author sound like a deep thinker. And that's exactly what it is; but since we don't have anything better to do (and if you do have anything better to do, I heartily recommend that you go off and do it), let's take that as read and find out where this excursion leads.

The G in AGA syndrome stands for grumpiness, mid-way between the A for Anger that you feel when you are young, and the A for Acquiescence you feel when you realise it's all gone to hell and there is nothing you can do about it. That middle phase between Anger and Acquiescence is Grumpiness, and that's what this book is all about.

How does it work? Well, when you are growing up – especially for a certain type of man – you are in a tearing hurry. Everything you want to do, you want to do now. Nothing happens fast enough for you. The people in the supermarket are moving their trolleys too slowly, while you know what you want and you're banging your trolley against the back of their heels trying to get around fast enough. When you come out of the supermarket, you are in a bad temper. You drive your car far too fast through the car park, nearly send your family through the roof as you bump over the sleeping policemen, almost run down the old couple whose heels you were banging into half an hour ago, and probably blast your horn. You are in a hurry, hurry, hurry. What are these people waiting for? Get the hell out of my way!

Everyone else hates being in a car with you because you are always blasting the horn or shouting at people out of the window. To compensate for lost time you have had to multi-skill. For your dad this meant drinking tea and reading the paper at the same time. For you it means driving the car while answering your texts, listening to Radio 5 Live, talking on the phone about the latest cash-flow forecasts, reading the map and eating a high-fibre and perfectly balanced muesli bar. When email came along it was a blessing because it allowed you to read and answer messages while drinking tea, studying the contract on your desk, sending a text, and holding a conference call with New York, Singapore and Oswestry at the same time.

You were in such a hurry that you ran up escalators, paced up and down when the lift didn't arrive on time, puffing and blowing, tapping on the walls and pressing and re-pressing the already illuminated button, and meanwhile seeing if this was another opportunity to take a phone call or send a text consisting entirely of consonants because vowels are so lst cntry (*sic*).

You drank too much coffee, got more and more hyper, and damn nearly had a heart attack when your wife asked if you could just drop Amanda off at her flute lesson on your way to the airport.

And since nothing worked the way you wanted it – the kids didn't do as they were told, the promotion didn't come along fast enough, the traffic didn't clear to make a path for you, the plane was late – you spent a good deal of your time angry.

Angry young men. The first A in AGA. Wake up at the back. We'll return to G for Grumpiness in a minute and skip straight on to A for Acquiescence.

When you are quite a bit older, back end of your 50s, with retirement looming or even upon you, we have to hope that you have mellowed. You've had a lot of old nonsense to put up with – obnoxious boss, stroppy kids, a wife who didn't do exactly what you wanted whenever you wanted, but by and large you got through it reasonably unscathed. Life may not have worked out exactly as you had in mind, but, hey, this is probably as good as it's going to get. This is the age when you can start to feel a bit smug.

When you hear predictions that the big cities are expected to reach total gridlock by 2015, you shake your head sympathetically with your younger colleagues, while secretly thinking, 'What do I care? Let them rot. I'm out of here.'

When you hear about global warning, you have to pretend to be concerned because of the kids, but all the time you're thinking, 'Thank God for that.

I wonder if I could have a go at growing some grapes on the back patio.'

You reckon you've done your bit, done your best, and the world has still all turned to horse dung. You are sorry that it didn't work out better, but if you are really honest, you can't be arsed to be all that sorry. You are mellow. Chilled, I think the young people of today call it. Acquiescent.

So, to summarise, you're angry when you are young because you are in a hurry and things rarely work out exactly as you want them; and you are acquiescent when you are old mainly because you are relieved to have 'got away with it'. In between those two stages you are grumpy: 35–54 is the core age group – the Republican Guard of Grumpy Old Men.

You have left behind the feeling when you grab the parking ticket off the windscreen that you want to hunt down the traffic warden and make him eat it, but are not quite at the point where you sigh and tuck it neatly in your pocket for immediate payment. You're at the stage where you peel the ticket off the window, fix it with a withering stare and mutter, 'Thank you, God, that's another great start to another great big arse of a day' before getting on about your business.

You are grumpy. Everything around you pisses you off. Everywhere you look the world has conspired to get under your skin. The weather is too hot, too cold, or too mild. Too wet or too dry. The government is too extreme, too moderate, or too boring. Your kids are getting on your nerves, or they are not getting on your nerves at the moment, but that's only because they are regrouping for the next phase of driving you up the wall. Your boss is probably younger than you, and is getting above himself. You are desperate to tell him to insert the job where the sun doesn't shine, but you don't have nearly enough in the retirement fund. And, anyway, the investments are all going backwards. All the time you were paying your mortgage

interest rates were above 10 per cent. Now you're close to paying it off and maybe have a few quid in the bank, they're down at 4 per cent. Meanwhile, your endowment mortgage is worth about half what they promised it would be, so bang goes the second home in Polperro.

On the telly there is nothing but bloody rubbish, and the wife wants you to take her to Sorrento for the holidays. Every day you pick up the newspapers there is another story about some criminally incompetent boss picking up a golden parachute big enough to float you down gently into your dream of early retirement. You're appalled that footballers are earning £100,000 a week and seem to think it's OK to shag every 17-year-old girl they set eyes on, and all that wouldn't be so bad if the team was not also crap.

This is the age when people stop asking you, 'What have you been up to?' and start asking, 'How have you been?' When a phone call at ten at night isn't likely to be an invitation to a party, but more likely to be news that a schoolmate has had a heart attack.

Recognise anything here? Do any three of the above apply to you? Yep, sounds like you are one of us.

Now you could of course be a woman or a young person reading this book because you are full of concern about your loved one – your partner or your dad. Is he a Grumpy Old Man, and if so how can you help him? Well, if this is you, take heart. This is one of the very few occasions where I can give you a cast-iron guarantee. If you are in any doubt at all about whether the man about the house is a Grumpy Old Man, he isn't. Because if you have one, you know it. There can be no mistake.

Women who are married to one know it without question. I've heard the same thing from women dozens of times in the last few months. No ifs, no buts – the minute the subject is mentioned, 'Oh, I've got one of those at home,' and it's said with all the finality that would characterise a statement that the dog was a Highland terrier. 'Not a Scottie?' 'What, do you think I don't know my own dog?' As clear and unambiguous a statement as they could make. The old man is grumpy. Case closed.

And if you're a teenager or in your early 20s and your dad is one, my guess, just the same, is that you know it straight away. I've lost count of the number of 14–25-year-olds I've spoken to who told me they watched the TV series because they were always expecting their dads to appear.

'The old man is always going on about the same stuff,' I'd hear them whine, followed by an animated debate about whether their dad is more or less embarrassing than their friend's dad. 'You should see him trying to dance. I didn't

know where to look.' 'That's nothing, mine still buys his clothes at Top Man.' The litany of paternal sins then dissolves into a mélange in which the most frequently overheard word is 'saddo'.

So take heart. If you are a Grumpy Old Man, you can be in no doubt about it. If you are married to one, there will be no room for ambiguity. If your dad is one – well, it seems to me that most dads are. If you don't recognise any of the symptoms so far, you can relax. My advice is to put this book down and pick up a nice Joanna Trollope.

The only remaining concern is among male readers yet to reach their mid-30s, who may be worried about the symptoms to look out for, or for other readers who see the man about the house exhibiting no symptoms today, but are naturally worried about the future. Prevention, they say, is better than cure, which should not be taken to indicate that I believe grumpiness is subject to either prevention or cure. Nonetheless, for those of an optimistic disposition, the next chapter gives a few signs to watch out for.

CHAPTER 3

How do you know it's coming on?

It's not necessarily easy to identify the symptoms beyond doubt, especially if, as in my case, you have always had a predisposition towards the grumpy tendency.

For example, if people tend to say of you, 'He doesn't suffer fools gladly,' you may not yet be a Grumpy Old Man, but you sound a bit like a candidate. By the way, don't be tempted to take that remark about 'not suffering fools' as a compliment because what it really means is that you are an intolerant and impatient sod.

I believe that another characteristic is a tendency towards undue assertiveness – frequently totally unfounded – which becomes increasingly trenchant if challenged. And even more trenchant than that if wrong. Oddly enough, that's another one I've occasionally been accused of myself.

There may also be some physical implications. These are not essential, but perhaps they might provide some of the general environment against which grumpiness develops. For example, at a certain point it starts taking a bit longer to pee, and then you may not be pissing quite so lustily as you did in your 'eight pints a night' days. That's eight pints of beer, not piss, though I guess it probably amounts to the same thing.

Worse than that is having to get up in the night for a wee –
catastrophic to those of us already plagued by insomnia.

There's deteriorating eyesight. Lapses of concentration. And
repeating yourself. Also there are the lapses of concentration.
(Sorry – I tried, honest I did, but I couldn't resist it.)

But I think the first and only really unmistakable sign is
the gradual onset of the continuous running commentary
inside your head. Where once you might have had the capacity,
either through your own inner peace or a drug-induced stupor,
to empty your mind and allow it to wander unencumbered
by the flotsam and jetsam of everyday life, increasingly you
find that you are a prisoner in your own consciousness.
Unwelcome and frankly unattractive thoughts keep coming
at you with increasing relentlessness, until they join up into a
fast-flowing stream.

And once it really starts, it never leaves you alone. For years.

On the train, you are actively listening out for the
announcements so that you can find something to grumble
about. 'The next station-stop is Rugby.' When they hear this, all
the Grumpy Old Men on the train who would be better off
getting a life are instead off on an unstoppable mental rant that
goes something like this: 'Why isn't that "The next station is
Rugby" or "The next stop is Rugby"? Now I come to think
about it, I suppose I can see why they can't say, "The next stop
is Rugby" because if the train then stops at a red light and
someone gets out thinking they're at Rugby and plummets into
the path of an oncoming express, they'll sue the railway for
every penny the taxpayer has put in through subsidy. And now
I come to think about it, I can see why they can't say, "The next
station is Rugby" because there may be a station between here
and Rugby but at which we are not stopping.'

So you end up reluctantly agreeing with the ridiculous
formula 'The next station-stop is Rugby', by which time you've

missed the next announcement, which is the one you needed to hear.

Watching the telly, you're mentally satirising the men for their ridiculous haircuts: 'I wonder how long it took him to look that much of a woofter?' You're appraising the women for their unwise outfits: 'Doesn't she realise that that top makes her look as though she's six months pregnant?' or 'Why does she think it's OK to read the news with her tits hanging out?'

When the earnest reporter is talking to us outside 10 Downing Street, all we're doing is watching the people coming in and out of that big black door and waiting and hoping that the pizza delivery boy will arrive and call out, 'Who ordered pepperoni?' 'Pepperoni?' A jerk of the thumb to the right. 'That's for the Scots git next door.'

Or we're watching the face of the policeman standing outside Number 10 as he tries to pretend he hasn't noticed that there is a reporter standing right next to him with cameraman, sound recordist, lights and an idiot researcher. Why do people do that?

Or we're looking at the classroom of kids working away quietly in the background of the reporter's 'piece to camera', and you know that the producer has said, 'Just pretend we're not here,' as if it's an everyday occurrence to have a TV crew in the lesson. And who knows, maybe it is.

We're monitoring the weather forecast, listening out for phrases such as 'more organised bands of rain coming in from the west' so that we can point out that rain doesn't come in bands, and, if it did, they couldn't be organised. And we're even further irritated if there is no one around to point this out to. As if they'd be even remotely interested.

Occasionally we might have seen about 45 trailers for a new drama on the telly and think we'll give it a chance to grab our interest, but we're going to spoil it for everyone around us by finding it so full of clichés that we'll sit there supplying the next line of script before the actor does – and as often as not we're going to be right.

When an interviewer asks an interviewee, 'How frightened were you?' we're always going to supply the answer, 'Very frightened' just before they do. When they ask, 'How worried are you?' we're uncannily accurate in responding on their behalf, 'Very worried'. When they ask the mother of a dead child, 'How do you feel?' we're going to ask, 'How the hell do you think she feels, you prat?'

Yes, when we're watching *Top of the Pops* to see if they have any scantily clad dancers on this week, we're genuinely appalled by the fact that no one can play an instrument and none of the songs will ever be able to be sung on coach trips. Remember 'We All Live in a Yellow Submarine'? I don't think the charabanc trips to Morecambe of the future will be resounding to 'Smack My Bitch Up' or 'Suck On This Hoe', do you?

And just what is going on with these rappers grabbing their crotches the whole time? With most physical things – tattoos, piercings, strange shapes carved into the scalp – we may not appreciate it but on some level we 'get it'. Holding your crotch while dancing? Beats the hell out of me.

Increasingly, as we go through our everyday lives, we see bullshit wherever we go, and we are less and less tolerant of it.

Where once I would look at the poor sod standing on the street corner with a yellow sash and collecting tin and think, 'Better put something in the box' or, more likely, suddenly become apparently mesmerised by a bird on the guttering high up in the other direction, now all I'm thinking is, 'Yet another bastard trying to take money off me.' Where once the legions of foreign students approaching me on the pavement and asking, 'Can you spare a moment for the homeless?' would have received the reply, 'No, sorry, I'm afraid I'm in a hurry,' nowadays

I just look them in the eye with an expression that's meant to convey, 'Do I look like a totally credulous halfwit to you?' and dares them to mess with me for a single moment longer.

So these are some of the signs to look out for in yourself and your loved ones. Generally increasing intolerance, especially of shopkeepers and young people. A greater willingness to be obnoxious to call-centre staff and anyone trying to sell you anything. A tendency to see the ridiculous in everything new, from daft ringtones to the studio of *ITV News*. A tendency to answer, 'Yeah, right' when anyone tries to persuade you that something has improved, and a blanket 'Get out of my face' response to anyone who invades your personal space.

It's not very attractive, is it? But my guess is that if you think you recognise yourself in any of the above, this may be a dangerous book for you to read. In the next chapter we're going to reveal the full and undiluted grumpy experience through an average day, and it's not for the faint-hearted. If you are one of those people who would prefer not to know what the future holds, as they say on the telly before revealing the football score, 'Look away now'. If you choose to read on...well, don't say I didn't warn you.

CHAPTER 4

So what are we grumpy about?

When I see this chapter heading at the top of the page all I can think of is, 'Don't get me started', but I guess if we don't get started on what Grumpy Old Men are grumpy about, there won't be much point in this book. But 'Don't get me started' isn't just an irritating turn of phrase, though of course it is that as well. No, though most people who know one will find this very difficult to believe, Grumpy Old Men aren't necessarily very comfortable 'going on about it'.

I know, I know, what on earth am I talking about? 'All you Grumpy Old Men ever seem to do is go on about it.' And while there may be some truth in that, the truly scary thing is the amount of time we just think it and don't actually say it. It's all going on in our heads, but because we are alone, can't be bothered, or sense that we are becoming even more irritating than the patience of any reasonable human being can tolerate, it stays there.

In fact, I'd say the ratio of grumbles that stay in my head to the ones that actually gain expression probably runs at about 50:1. Which can only mean that my brain is racing at about 100 miles per hour with stuff, and also probably makes me a very sick and sad individual.

The best way to tell you what Grumpy Old Men are actually grumpy about is to take you through a typical day. So welcome to my world...

START AS YOU MEAN TO GO ON

'The minute you leave your house in the morning you see something that makes you grumpy.'

ARTHUR SMITH

There's undoubtedly a lot of truth in that: however, in my case it really starts a whole hell of a lot earlier. It starts reliably some time before I'm fully awake, because I tend to come around gradually to the sound of the BBC World Service.

Now to be fair, there's not all that much about the World Service from about 5 a.m. onwards that irritates me. Grumpies who suffer from the same early-morning tendencies will know that it's not a bad round-up of world events – and it's always interesting to get a take on the news that doesn't necessarily start with disruption of the trains in the Midlands and end with the break-up of S Club 7 or 6 or however many there are left. Especially on days when 20,000 people have been killed in an Iranian earthquake.

No, the problem with the World Service arises if you wake up at 3 a.m., which I not infrequently do, and turn on the radio to help you stop thinking about all the things that will inevitably make you depressed at that time of the morning. Depression comes all too easily then. So much so that I've now had to make it a personal life rule to remember that anything I think at three in the morning must be bollocks, merely by virtue of the fact that it is three in the morning.

This is a digression, but it lays the foundation for the typical day in the life of a grumpy.

The reason I know that anything I think of at three in the morning must be bollocks is because I used to get what I always thought were my best ideas at that time. They were so good that they were certain to make me a multi-millionaire and change the world for the better. The only trouble was that I'd always forgotten them by the time dawn eventually came around. How could I have forgotten such a great idea? And if I did eventually think I'd remembered it, I'd be sure I couldn't have got it right because the idea I remembered was nowhere near as good as the one I'd had four hours earlier. If only I could properly remember it. Are you still with me?

This was plainly such a huge loss that I resolved to put a pencil and paper beside the bed. I did this for a few weeks, secure in the knowledge that now the only problem would be how to find enough hours in the day properly to exploit all my great ideas at the same time. I'd turn the idea round in my mind for half an hour or so in the small hours, until it was so life-enhancing that the only remaining question was how to clear enough shelf space for yet another Nobel prize. Then I'd pop on the bedside light ever so briefly and scribble down a few words on a scrap of paper. This would enable me to attempt to go back to sleep, confident that the good people of the world were not going to be robbed of the fruits of my moment of inspiration.

What I quickly found was that, in the cold light of day, I'd look at the crumpled piece of paper by my bed, try hard to decipher the scrawl, and wonder what on earth I could have been thinking of. 'Underground car parks in Venice?' What could I have had in mind? Anyway, turns out I never have a good idea in the middle of the night that still seems to be one five hours later.

It's chemical. Something goes wrong in the small hours with your biorhythms or whatever they are, substituting your ordinary powers of analysis for the intellectual rigour of Ronald

McDonald. The silver lining to this cloud is that this is the same with depression. The same chemistry that percolates stupid ideas in your head in the small hours of the morning also makes you think the worst about everything. Now I'm fortunate in not being naturally a depressive sort of person. Grumpy, yes, but depressive, no. But quite a few times over the last ten years I've reached the view in the middle of the night that the only sensible course of action is suicide.

Try as I might, I just can't really see any other way out, so the obvious thing to do is to end it all. I even start planning the means to the end. A lot of pills and brandy, I think, rather than anything violent or too undignified. Then when I wake up properly in the morning I cannot for the life of me imagine what I was thinking. Sure, there are a few things I've got to sort out, but nothing remotely that bad. And therefore, I've now made a note to myself that anything I think in the middle of the night, good or bad, is bollocks. It's amazing what a relief that is. You should try it.

This is a long (and more intimate than I had intended) way of telling you why it is that I tend to lean over and put the radio on if I wake up in the early hours. I'm hoping that the programme will be just interesting enough to stop me thinking that I've invented a new way to transport people across London by fax or, at the other extreme, that I've got my life savings in the equivalent of BCCI and am going to wake up with nothing to show for all these years of conscientious toil and be condemned to an old age of penury.

I need something that is just interesting enough to keep away other thoughts, but not so interesting that I want to stay awake to hear more of it. A sort of perpetual radio version of *Countdown*.

Instead of that, all too frequently I turn on at the moment that John Peel, God bless him, is giving airtime to the just unbelievably dreadful, cacophonous nonsense that is obviously sent to him routinely and to which, being a very good bloke, he feels it would be nice to give some airtime. Actually, on reflection, I think it's a bit worse than that. John Peel is indeed a very nice bloke, who might well play the record (or whatever you call it these days) just to give five tone-deaf lads making a din in the garage a chance of being heard by an A & R man in Bangalore. However, I suspect that's not the real reason. I suspect that John actually does it because he is the only person in Britain, nay in the whole world, who really enjoys this dreadful racket. John enjoys all sorts of stuff, from the very, very good to the very, very awful, and is genuinely happy to listen to it at home, and then play it with real enthusiasm to the unsuspecting world at what is, after all, peak time in the Falklands. Or somewhere.

All well and good, and good luck to the Grunge or the Syphilitic Scrotes or whatever the five putrid lads in the garage are called, but this doesn't solve it for me. I don't want to listen to it, and I certainly cannot go to sleep to it. So I have to turn it off, and then it's back to my thoughts, which may be about selling up and moving lock, stock and barrel to the Orkneys, or about how the griping pain in my abdomen must be an embryonic alien and it's my inevitable fate to cut it out before it can give birth to itself through the walls of my intestines and wreak havoc across the world. OK, I know I'm off on one, but this is less of an exaggeration than you might think.

Then there is *Westway*. Again, insomniacs won't need to be told that this is an everyday story of a medical centre, though I've never heard it sufficiently regularly to register an extended storyline or indeed a location. I suspect that it may be in the international equivalent of Ambridge. What it is, however, is the most ham-fisted and patronising drivel, exemplifying everything that is bad about the neo-colonialism of the World Service.

The cast of *Westway* are always having ethical dilemmas; they're always interfering to try to get Grandpa to recognise and forgive the fact that someone in the family is gay or has AIDS. Or giving nauseatingly liberal perspectives on things such as arranged marriages, on the one hand understanding why it's good to be obedient to parents and to adhere to the time-honoured culture of families, but at the same time gently hinting that it's the twenty-first century and maybe it's not a bad idea to give a woman some small say in who shags her. And maybe, since she's still only 12, it shouldn't be anyone at all. For five or six years anyway.

Whoever writes this odious nonsense obviously has a mental picture of an ageing old twot in a turban listening intently by his wind-up radio, fingering his beard, furrowing his brow and thinking, 'Maybe I should be more broad-minded after all. Then I can live like these people in Ambridge.' He then goes off and forgives Raffi, or whatever he's called, and they all live happily ever after. All thanks to the great white Auntie across the water.

And then, there is all the branding on the World Service these days. All that 'Brought to you by the BBC…' and 'The BBC has learnt…' and 'The BBC's man in…' It's 'BBC this' and 'BBC that' every two minutes. Now this is relatively new, but for the last couple of years they've alighted on a house style that has six or seven different voices with different accents saying, 'This is the BBC in Kabul' and then 'This is the BBC in Addis Ababa' and then 'This is the BBC in Nairobi' and so on, followed by an oleaginous voice saying, 'Wherever you are, however you listen, this is the BBC.' Now this promotion, variations of which pop up hundreds and hundreds of times a day, doesn't make sense. In fact I've heard it so often that I almost think it does make sense. 'Wherever you are, however you listen, this is the BBC'? What on earth are you talking about?

So what with the astonishingly bad music, the appalling scripts of the drama, the dreadful and continuing self-congratulation for being the BBC, I'm likely to be grumpy well before I wake up properly. However, by 5.30 a.m. I'm irretrievably and irredeemably awake, and ready for a new day.

OVER THE AIRWAVES

'I'm sure they have a special screening where they go, "I'm sorry but you don't appear to be a nutter, so we can't actually put you on the air." Any debate about war or dictators will go straight to Hitler. Or any debate about technology will go straight to "Well, we've put a man on the moon." There's actually a rule in the BBC Charter which says that only people talking in total clichés are allowed to be put in these programmes.' JOHN O'FARRELL

It probably starts with the Radio 4 UK theme. This is a brilliantly conceived and marvellously executed orchestral medley of tunes from all over Britain – seamlessly merging 'Greensleeves' with 'Rule Britannia' via 'Men of Harlech' and a swift 'Sailor's Hornpipe'. I think they've drawn the line at 'Jerusalem', but only because it didn't sit well with a jaunty beat. Now this was OK the first time, and it wasn't too bad the fifth time. By the twentieth time I heard it, I'd sort of got my head around it and was beginning to get a bit irritated. But this bloody anthem plays at the same time every day, yes I mean every single day, of life. At about 5.32 a.m. Exactly the same piece, at exactly the same time, every single day of life.

I thought of writing in, but I knew I'd be wasting my time. I'd get one of those patronising and word-processed letters back that assured me that they try to cater for a wide range of taste and interests, and that this particular anthem was a key point in the day for many of their listeners. They had the letters to prove it.

When Greg Dyke got the job of director general, I determined to mention it to him, but somehow I never got around to it, and now it's too late. In any event, scrapping the Radio 4 UK theme would probably have cost him his job far more quickly and with far more blood than committing the heinous crime of standing up for his staff too quickly.

Day after day I lie there, more or less in suspended animation, until *Prayer for the Day* comes on, swiftly followed by *Farming Today*. Now *Prayer for the Day* I quite like. In it some usually harmless old buffer gives a more or less spiritual spin on world events. This is one of the few moments of the day, in these secular times we live in, when someone on radio or television is allowed to mention God. The highest accolade I can pay to it is that I rarely find myself tut-tutting.

Farming Today, however, is another matter. This is one of those programmes that has decided that the ordinary business of running a farm is far too boring for a radio programme, so it takes the position that everything is a 'poison time-bomb waiting to go off' or 'set to destroy a way of life for thousands of farmers up and down the land'. Chemical residues, it turns out, have been seeping towards the water-table for years and have now been found to cause buboes in field mice. This morning it was 'British farmers may lose their entitlement to grants and be cast into the outer darkness for eternity if they make a single elementary clerical slip-up in filling out the application forms.' There's lots of very excitable 'We've uncovered...' going on, and a great deal of secretive 'We've been told that...' Time and again, morning after morning, the indignant interviewer is stridently giving a hard time to whoever is the current hapless minister.

'But why hasn't the government done something about it?' she cries. 'We have done something about it,' he answers. 'But not enough,' she explodes. 'We think it is enough.' He is getting more exasperated. 'It isn't working.' 'Yes, it is working.' 'We've spoken to people who say it isn't.' 'Well, we're working very closely with people who say that it is.' 'Who's that?' 'I'm not telling you.' And all the while he's thinking, 'I wonder how much longer I've got to put up with this abuse before Tony gives me a proper job.' Better ask Nick Brown.

I go on to listen to the *Today* programme because, although it irritates me almost beyond endurance, it irritates me less than any other radio news I have been able to find. I think this must be even worse for me than for most grumpies because I have a bit of a background in broadcasting. However, it can't only be me who, when hearing, 'That's all we've got time for' thinks this actually means: 'We're incompetent bastards who don't really know what we're doing. This was a very interesting piece, and there's far more that is important and fascinating that we could be saying about it, but because the editor has insisted that we have a bit of light and shade in the programme, we have to cut it short so that we can interview the mad vicar of Throckley who does his shoelaces up the wrong way round. Therefore, we haven't got time to continue with the item you were interested in, and are ending it just as it was getting to the good bit.'

I guess you can see why 'That's all we've got time for' is used in preference.

Then, as often as not, having left a fascinating discussion that has just got going and promises to be a scorcher, we do indeed go to an interview with the mad vicar of Throckley who does his shoelaces up the wrong way round. And I'm left with a mental picture of the poor sod in the studio who, having had his intestines metaphorically ripped out by John Humphries and laid before the nation for microscopic scrutiny, was just managing to get to his point, and was cut off – only then to hear the airtime filled with the mad vicar.

The one real redeeming feature of Radio 4 is that, with a few exceptions, the presenters on it don't pretend that they are your mates. There's not a lot of 'I don't know about you but when I got up this morning…', which leaves you thinking, 'No, you don't know about me, do you? And you don't care about me either. In fact, you probably care about me just as much as I care about you. Which is sod all.'

The basic problem here is that there are just far too many radio stations, and far too much airtime, for the worthwhile material available to fill them. And also there just isn't enough talent in the whole wide world to occupy the thousands of presenters' seats there must be in local radio stations up and down the country, and that's not to mention BBC Radio 7. So these stations are obliged to fill the airwaves any way they can, and are therefore often left little choice but to do so with total plonkers.

Worst of all are the adenoidal reporters, mostly drafted in on attachment from BBC local radio in Stoke-on-Trent, Southampton or Stoke Poges, who've heard other people on the radio and think this is how you have to speak when you are a reporter. In clichés, with that all too familiar cadence that goes up at the start of the sentence and down at the end, whatever the sense: 'The jury heard that Mr Rodney Fisher, aged 56 from East Molesey, was on his way home when he was caught up in fighting between two gangs of youths. Mr Fisher was attacked with a blunt instrument and hit by flying missiles. He sustained serious head injuries and later died in hospital. Police have issued a photo-fit picture of the man they want to question. He is said to be 5 ft 10 inches tall, with black hair and a pale complexion. They have warned that he shouldn't be approached and should be considered as dangerous.'

Leave aside the fact that when I hear the word 'blunt instrument' I think of a tuba. Leave aside that when I hear 'flying missiles' I think of Trident. Leave aside that people very rarely die from trivial head injuries – I can probably work out from the fact that poor Mr Fisher died that the injuries were serious. Leave aside the fact that the description isn't worth the breath it takes to utter it. Leave aside that in the unlikely event that we see a man of 5 ft 10 carrying a bloodstained crowbar we'll probably know not to approach him. None of that irritates me beyond endurance. What does irritate me beyond endurance is that bloody ridiculous sing-song voice. Through their noses and with the same rhythm, line after line, story after story – happy, sad, human interest or industrial espionage.

This is a long way of saying that about ten past six, when I've heard the sweet, syrupy and sumptuous Charlotte Green read the news, I get up and go downstairs. The central heating sounds like the engine room of the *African Queen*, minus a sweaty Humphrey Bogart shovelling coal into it. But I suppose that's not surprising because, after all, the boiler must be at least 18 months old, so I know the next time the plumber turns up he'll be scratching his head and doubting if it's possible to get a spare part for a model this ancient.

Last time he came, and this is the God's honest truth, he looked into the boiler cupboard at the Medusa-like tangle of pipes and old lagging and asked, 'Who on earth fitted this?' My wife just did not know how to tell him that the answer was, 'You did, less than a year ago.' And, by the way, I have to say this in case he's a reader, he's the best plumber we've ever had. Oh, and if you're reading this Mr Riley, could you pop back and fix the leak in the outside tap?

So into the kitchen to put the kettle on. Nowadays we've got a green plastic kettle that makes a terrible noise from the moment you turn it on, and then changes colour as the water boils. I thought that was quite an entertaining novelty the first time I saw it. Now the flick of the switch seems to be enough to tell me that the water has boiled. Maybe the colour change is for the hard of hearing.

BREAKFAST TELEVISION

'Well, I suppose the media is such a major industry now, and it needs feeding, so rather than wait for celebrity to happen, they sort of invent it in order to report on it. Do you know what I mean? You don't necessarily have to wait any more. You just make it up as you go along.'
                                              BILL NIGHY

I put on the telly and usually tune to GMTV. Nothing against Dermot Murnahan and Natasha Kaplinsky, except that they are both too damned well turned out and perfect for that time of the morning. I think that first thing you want someone who looks just a little bit more like you feel. That's why I'm a bit more comfortable with John Stapleton – because he looks slightly more lived in. I also quite like Penny Smith because, although she's as mad as a box of frogs, there's something about her. Alan Lewens tells me that it's probably because she looks as though she enjoys sex. This may tell us more about Alan than it does about Penny.

But here's what gets up my nose about these programmes. 'We now go over to our political correspondent who is outside 10 Downing Street.' What is the point of that? It's ten past six on a freezing cold morning. It's lashing down with rain and the wind is blowing a gale. The poor woman – who has only two coats, both with unwise collars – is reporting on a story that has had no developments for the last eight hours, and won't have any more for the next six. Yet she has to stand with the prime minister's house in the background. Why? Do we think the PM might be watching, and be so irritated and excited by what she is saying that he'll pop on his dressing gown, scurry down the stairs and come out to put her right? Do we think we might see Osama Bin Laden being snuck in under cover of darkness for a tête-à-tête?

Of course we don't. It's a visual aid – because viewers are deemed to be so irredeemably dim that they need a shot of the door of Number 10 in the background to be able to keep in mind that this is a story about politics. Politics. Downing Street. Geddit?

You see it all over the place. Outside the offices of ACAS eight hours after the talks have ended and three hours before they are due to begin. Outside Heathrow because 'a plane like the one behind me' was forced to stage an emergency landing. And out in a street somewhere it's taken five hours to drive to because crime is increasing 'in streets like these'. Why won't they let these poor sods in out of the rain?

What I find even funnier is when there is a story in a place they can't send a reporter to, either because it's only just happened or because it's too hostile, so we go over to our reporter in the country next door. The most recent example was going over to John Stapleton in Kuwait because he couldn't get much closer to the war in Iraq.

Now London is probably the centre of the world communications network. There is hardly a picture, piece of film or agency report that doesn't tip up instantly on screens in

BBC TV Centre, or Reuters or ITN or the World Service. Kuwait, most assuredly, is not the centre. So you can be very certain that almost anything John Stapleton can tell you from Kuwait has been told to him 15 minutes earlier by someone in London. The same is true, but more so, in trying to report what's going on in Zimbabwe from South Africa. When you are in Johannesburg you just feel very centrally positioned – smack bang in the middle of nowhere – and for all practical purposes you are much further out of touch with the action in Harare than you would be in White City or the Gray's Inn Road.

It's about the equivalent of CBS not being able to send a reporter to London, so sending him to Reykjavic because that will make them look a little closer to where it's at. It's bollocks. It's just that having our correspondent apparently close to the action feels a bit macho. They think it gives an impression of gravitas and authority if we get to see our presenters in their safari outfits or flak jackets. Is that the impression it has on you? Whenever I see a reporter with a bulletproof vest over his chest, I'm just expecting to see a bullet hit him in the head.

Although I generally think they're a fairly professional lot on all the morning channels, this is probably my worst time of day, so my bullshit antennae are at maximum sensitivity. Recently I heard a reporter referring to a burglar's 'fatal error' in leaving his DNA at the scene, and found myself muttering, 'Who died?' People are always doing everything 'at this moment in time' rather than 'now'. No report is anything other than 'in-depth'. No insight is less than 'profound'. No crisis anything less than 'serious' – what kind of crisis isn't serious? Every problem is 'spiralling out of control'. Every fire is a 'blaze'. Every rescue is 'heroic'. Every death from cancer follows 'a brave struggle'. Every day when a tragedy occurred was 'that fateful day'. No report is less than 'damning'.

Today it is the 18th birthday of Charlotte Church, and

apparently we have an exclusive interview with her in which she talks frankly about her life and loves. Now of course I know who Charlotte Church is, but equally obviously I have no interest whatsoever in her. I'm vaguely aware that she was a child star, has the 'voice of an angel' and has fallen out with her mother or her manager or someone. However, slightly to my own surprise, I have gradually found myself feeling sorry for this kid. She's very young, she seems to be a complete airhead, and she is very, very rich. And that seems to be enough to make it all right for the news media of the world to regard every aspect of her personal life as public property. So there is enormous speculation about her love life, her sex life, and her wealth and what she might want to do with it.

Eventually we cut to the much-trailed interview with Charlotte Church and there she is, apparently being pressed into a corner and asked a series of impertinent questions about her boyfriends and what she plans to spend her money on. The idiot child is wincing and obviously embarrassed, and all she can say is, 'Don't believe everything you read in the papers', 'No, that's all nonsense', and 'I'll just be doing what any other 18-year-old would be doing – having a party with my mates.'

Now I'm always a bit torn when I see this. Half of me is saying, 'Why did you agree to give an interview if you weren't going to say anything?' and the other half of me is saying, 'Poor kid, fancy having to put up with all these jackasses asking you such personal questions. Tell them to sod off.' I don't know what you call this, but what it cannot possibly be described as, of course, is an interview in which she talks frankly about her life and loves.

Then we go over to the regional news and, since I'm watching in London, we're being brought right up to date with the various obstructions they've come up with to prevent us from getting to work today. The current presenter seems pleasant enough, but she thinks it's OK to wear her hipster jeans and show off part of her stomach when she's delivering the traffic information. She does, her editor obviously does, but I don't.

I'm always fascinated by the 'human wallpaper' of people facing computer screens just in the background of the luscious presenter. One of them looks very much as though he might be John Stapleton's twin brother. Another one looks a bit like an axe murderer. I imagine their mums tuning in every morning to see 'our Geoffrey' and being ever so proud that he's on the telly, but wishing he'd wear a tie and have a proper haircut. I know I do.

Back on the sofa they are doing an item about someone who gave up their job and set off around the world. 'And if you hate your job or just wish you could do something else, we'd love to hear from you. Why not log on to our website or send us a text?' What? If you hate your job, we'd love to hear from you? What are we supposed to imagine happens now? Thousands of people go to their mobiles and send a text to GMTV with a variation of 'I'm a time-management consultant and I bloody well hate it.' So what? Who gives a toss? And do these people ever wonder why GMTV would 'love to hear from them'? Because they get a rake-off from the price of the text, of course. And what happens? In about half an hour the presenters will read out two texts from an underpaid teacher in Burnley and an overworked dinner lady in Gateshead and all the rest go in the electronic recycle bin. And do you know what the astonishing thing is? That thousands of people actually do text in response to this utterly banal bullshit. What does that tell you?

Lastly, there is of course the weather forecast. Now once again, I don't have much of a problem with this in the morning. Both of the GMTV weather presenters seem OK: quite bright, quite presentable, taking it in turns to be pregnant, and considering how much airtime they have to fill, they don't talk too much drivel about the drizzle.

There is of course a bit of a tradition of glamorous breakfast TV presenters, of whom the most famous is the fabulous Ulrika Jonsson, but that really is a 'don't get me started' area. No, the one who makes me want to drill out my own brains is Sian Lloyd. You know, the Welsh woman with the square face, very straight fringe and a bit of a red tint going on. No doubt a very warm and kind person, but honestly, where do you even start? The funny thing is that she's been doing her extraordinarily affected accent and strangely balletic hand movements for so long that I think we've all become used to them. We've lost track of just how weird they are. But take an objective look, stand back and watch, and her performance just makes your jaw drop. What on earth does she think she's doing?

'That band of rain will coming s-w-e-e-p-i-n-g in from the west…' and her outstretched hand comes s-w-e-e-p-i-n-g in from the side of the screen, and then does a strange flip of the wrist, halfway between a flamenco dancer and a magician. All of which would be bad enough if sometimes the weather was actually forecast right.

Is there any other walk of life, anything else you can think of, where day after day, night after night, you sit and listen to someone telling you what is going to happen and it doesn't? Of course there isn't. Despite that, you still tune in religiously every day, just as though what they told you was worth listening to. If a City tipster was always wrong, you'd stop listening and he'd get the sack. Even horse-racing pundits presumably get it right a proportion of the time. Bloody astrologers get it right more often than the Met Office.

That's not what they'll tell you, though. No, ask the Met Office and they'll say they get their forecasts right something above 90 per cent of the time. Do they hell. They get it right for the same reason that fortune-tellers get it right. What they tell you is so vague and general that there's enough in there to enable them to argue that they were right, even when plainly wrong. 'Well, we did say there was a chance of a shower,' when it's been bucketing down with rain all afternoon.

About 25 years ago I was briefly one of those adenoidal reporters working for BBC local radio in Stoke-on-Trent, where they used to interrupt the morning music show with a live update from the newsroom, which ended with a 'quick look at the weather'. The news editor would outline various stories, then glance out of the window, look at the sky and say something such as, 'And the weather…dry with sunny periods, the chance of an odd shower later.' Whatever he said, he was more or less always right.

At the Met Office today they use millions and millions of

pounds of technology, hot-air balloons, weather satellites, measuring stations, you name it, and they get it right about as often as the news editor at BBC Stoke-on-Trent. Ask a farmer. Ask a fisherman. Hang up a lump of seaweed, but let's not all sit there slavishly listening to these guys day after day for anything other than the entertainment of wondering what on earth Michael Fish thinks he looks like in that ridiculous red jacket. Dressed like that, I'd be more inclined to give credibility to the weather forecast according to David Icke.

IN BLACK AND WHITE

'If you've worked in Fleet Street for a number of years, you've seen it all...particularly the kind of journalism I write, which a friend of mine called "ingenious bubble-wrap". You know, it's there for the people at home popping the little bubbles and going, "Oh pop, oh pop".'

WILL SELF

Around about now I hear the newspaper drop through the letter-box. Or rather I hear the newspaper dropping through the letter-box about five times because the poor sod who delivers it has to divide it into sections to squeeze it through our average-size opening.

Time was when your newspaper contained news. That seems like a very odd idea today, but people genuinely used to buy a paper to find out what had happened around the world. I know, weird isn't it? Mind you, those were the days before breakfast television, and before 24-hour news channels. TV news was on at lunchtime, 6 o'clock, and at 9 or 10 p.m. In those days, hard though it is to recall, news didn't seem like something that happened all the time, on a continuous basis.

We just relied on people we never heard about to filter out the stuff we needed to know or would find interesting, ditch the rest, and to tell us at some point that was convenient to them.

As a matter of fact, I used to do this myself. It was about the lowliest job in the newsroom – it was called 'copy-tasting' – and you used to have to read all the news stories that came over the wires from agencies around the world, and decide what was sufficiently interesting to draw to the attention of your editor. The (unwritten) rule of news interest went something like: 'One dead in Putney equals ten dead in Paris, equals 100 dead in Turkey, equals 1000 dead in India, equals 10,000 dead in China.' Or something like that. If you took a story with only 9000 dead in China to the editor of the day, he (and it was always 'he') would look at the copy, look at you as though you were the village idiot, turn his nose up and spike it.

Today, of course, there is none of that discretion or discrimination. The appetite for news is such that it just comes straight off the wires and goes straight on to the screen. We've become a nation of news junkies, getting our fix from dozens of TV channels and radio stations.

Then there's news online or news via your telephone. Just in case, horror of horrors, you should have to wait an hour to find out that the Edinburgh bin-men are planning a strike in three months' time, you can subscribe to a news service that will send text headlines direct to your mobile. A recent TV promotion for the service showed a series of brief examples of texts illustrating the service, the last of which said something like, 'Parents slammed by teachers...' I just can't help wondering who can possibly need to know so urgently about parents being slammed that they need to read it in a text message to their mobile. I wouldn't be even remotely interested if they had been slammed against a wall by a number 47 bus, let alone by teachers. And I think my life would go on if I had to wait an hour to find out.

To find out whether you are in danger of becoming a news junkie, try this simple test on yourself. Just do a quick analysis in the course of one news programme of the stuff you really needed to know. Or let's take an even wider and more generous definition and include stuff that would genuinely contribute towards you counting yourself as a 'better-informed person'. David Beckham has a new hairstyle, a new tattoo, a new personal assistant, or a new anything. Gordon Brown still wants to be prime minister. Kelly Maguire thinks she's pregnant. David Blunkett has pissed off the judges. About 70 per cent of it is utterly meaningless drivel, here today gone tomorrow, total bollocks that it doesn't make a shred of difference if you know or not. In fact, you're better off not knowing most of it because all it does is to hack you off.

Have you ever tried taking a fortnight's holiday and not reading the papers while you're away? In about five years' time someone will mention that a famous actor has died and you might have missed it. Other than that, your life goes on more or less as normal.

In any event, there is more than enough so-called news available instantly to ensure that anything printed in the newspapers six hours earlier is going to be out of date by the time we read it. Even now it's not that rare for us to see a headline in a daily newspaper that has been overtaken by events. I always assume that these are grim days in the newsrooms of those particular papers. Your front page screams, 'Queen Mother Teeters' and the whole world knows that she's already tottered. But maybe they don't care so long as they've sold the papers.

So faced with this redundancy of their traditional role, daily newspaper editors have had to change their game. Nowadays they rarely even bother to try to put news in the newspapers. Instead they fill their columns with sensational nonsense, total inventions, digitally altered pictures, spin, comment and the frequently entertaining but entirely content-free chit-chat of a wide range of very clever people. Indeed, the redundancy of news in newspapers has provided gainful employment for a whole variety of engaging and amusing people, of whom very little would otherwise have been heard.

Which reminds me: is it just me, or is the rest of the world also as irritated by bloody Anne Robinson? I used to quite like Anne Robinson before she became 'Anne Robinson'. Do you know what I mean? There is a long history of people whom we find quite engaging for some particular idiosyncrasy that they just have as part of their personality; which is fine until some know-all points out to them that this is what people find engaging about them, and then they start doing it self-consciously and drive you to distraction.

Do you remember Magnus Pyke? He was the original mad scientist, but he was so enthusiastic and excited about his subject that he used to wave his arms about. It was such a natural thing for him to do that we liked him for it. Then some idiot obviously told him, 'You know, the great thing about you, Magnus...' and he started waving his arms about like a bloody windmill even when otherwise relaxed. It made him look a prat. Instead of seeing a scientist who was so enthusiastic about his subject that he just couldn't keep his arms still, we started seeing a bloody lunatic with St Vitus' Dance.

A similar thing happened to David Bellamy. You remember, the very hairy one with no roof to his mouth who used to grab handfuls of mud and tell you what it felt like 'oozing' between his fingers. He eventually became a caricature of himself. Peter Snow was the same with his stupid sodding swingometer: a genuine enthusiast, who eventually turned himself into a laughing stock. Now I don't know if Anne's wink at the camera ever looked and felt a natural thing for her to do, but in any event it's now so mannered that it just makes you want to grab her scrawny neck, rip her surgically altered head off and pour drain-cleaner into the void.

How did we get on to Anne Robinson? Oh yes, her bloody column. Always splurging on about bloody Penrose this and Penrose that, as if we give a damn. And then there's Esther Rantzen. Of course we all love her, but over recent years Esther has confided to us via the *Daily Mail* rather more than many of us would wish to know about her intimate personal arrangements. For example, for some reason best known to herself, she decided that we'd be better off knowing that she likes to wear lace and silk next to her skin, and that she regularly runs round the garden stark naked 'except for a chiffon hat'. We are left to speculate on the reason for the hat – perhaps she think the neighbours might not realise it's her.

'Oh, there goes that mad woman running around naked in Esther's garden. I wonder if we should let her know.'

We have also learnt that Esther has given up her bloomers and taken to wearing thongs, and that 'as I dress and undress the thong shape lengthens the leg and flattens the tummy'. Now I really don't want to be ageist, but last time I looked Esther was into her sixties. Whatever happened to growing older gracefully? And to cap it all, yes this one takes the proverbial Bath Oliver, we were recently treated to Esther's favourable review on the 'orgasmatron', a new device developed by scientists in America and designed to produce an instant female orgasm at the touch of a button.

Now this is in the morning 'newspaper' and I'm reading it over my Shreddies. I just cannot be alone in this. I really would struggle to think of anything, I mean anything, I want to visualise less than Esther bloody Rantzen's thong, or anything to do with her views on the female orgasm. Loads of things in the daily paper turn my stomach – death and pestilence in foreign countries, stories of old folk being beaten up in their homes, anything about Michael Howard – but I really think that Esther Rantzen romping in the garden wearing only a chiffon hat takes the prize. How did it get to this?

And it's not just Esther. Good heavens, no. If it were, we could just sigh and resolve never again in any circumstances to pick up the *Mail*. But you can hardly pick up a newspaper without reading a celebrity review of the rampant rabbit or hysterical hare or whatever it's called. Articles on 'How to turn him on', 'How to turn him off', 'How to make him jealous', 'How to know if he's two-timing you', 'How to two-time him', and how to give him and his two mates a good time at the same time. I'm not sure if there's anyone anywhere simply having straightforward one-to-one sex in the missionary position and in the privacy of their own bedroom any more.

We seem to have subcontracted the whole business to pop stars, footballers and, heaven help us, footballers' wives.

Perhaps surprisingly, relatively few of us have totally given up the notion that we'll find something worth reading in the newspapers – otherwise we would also have given up buying them – so we seem to have developed our individual techniques for navigating our way through. For example, Alan Lewens tells me that he usually reads the first two paragraphs and decides on that basis whether to read on. I, on the other hand, always go straight to the third paragraph. This is because the first two paragraphs or so are always a variation of 'I don't know about you but…' This is one of several ways of filling a couple of column inches before getting to the main subject, which is going to be too thin on its own to fill the space the editor has obliged the columnist to fill. I assume that by the third paragraph we might at least be getting a hint about the actual subject. Usually I'm wrong, and I scan the rest of the piece for a sentence that actually states a fact, or something worth reading for some other reason, before giving up and looking for the crossword.

ANIMALS OF ALL PERSUASIONS

'You know, I have never deliberately run over a fox. They are always too quick for me. But dogs. I don't like dogs. Because owners always assume you like their dogs as much as they do.' RORY MCGRATH

Before making a grab for the Golden Grahams, allow me briefly to share with you something that is fresh in my mind because of a recent experience. Now I know that many of my contemporaries who cheerfully describe themselves as Grumpy

Old Men are very fond of dogs. 'They're so much more straightforward than people,' you will occasionally hear them say. Or, 'At least you can have a decent conversation with your dog' – whatever that means. 'They won't ever let you down – unlike humans.' How pitiable is that?

However, as you might have guessed by now, I do not share this benign view of our canine companions. Partly because of the very idea of dogs being 'companions'. It's a weird thing when you think about it – that members of one species keep members of another species alongside them for so-called companionship. Are humans the only species to do this? You don't see parrots keeping bees, do you? Or gorillas keeping aardvarks.

It would be good to be able to speculate that this apparent human need is a facet of our modern society with all its dysfunction and alienation, but I fear that this strange trait goes back a lot further than that. Indeed, this very morning I heard a report that a grave had been discovered dating back 9500 years in which a man had been buried with his cat. The report implied that this was the first-known example of man keeping a pet, whereas all I was thinking was that the relatives might have believed that the deceased would need a snack on the journey. In any event, let's spare the harebrained analysis and just say that I don't get it.

This doesn't mean that I object that other people do seem to get it. But whether you are a dog-lover, dog-indifferent or a dog-hater, you already know what I'm going to say. You already know it. What I object to is dogs coming up and sniffing at your crotch.

Now this horrible experience can be visited upon you in the street, or even in people's houses. I don't need to describe it because there isn't a single man reading this now who has not experienced it first hand. Quite often it will happen on a more or less deserted beach where you've gone for a quiet walk to contemplate the surf and the attractions of a John Stonehouse-like disappearance from the daily yoke. (You remember. Labour MP. Left a pile of clothes on a beach and turned up months later in Australia. With his secretary. Bit of a babe. Sheila something or other…)

You can see it coming from miles away. A large grey-spotted mutt with slobbering jaws, great acceleration and lousy brakes sees you in the distance and sets off in your direction. With almost uncanny speed, doubling in size every three seconds, it then comes bounding up to you with no apparent intention of stopping when it arrives. Its nose is pointed like a cruise missile with a nuclear warhead at your most private parts and it doesn't even hesitate as the distance closes to zero.

If you are a bloke, you know what you do next. You perform that very inelegant swivel, where your hips go to one side and one leg raises slightly, to give your most tender areas

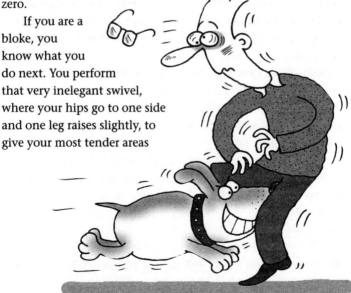

what little protection is available – short of falling prostrate, which might in itself have even more unlooked-for consequences. Indeed, it might be interpreted by the dog as acquiescence, nay, almost an invitation.

In the far distance the owner may or may not be shouting at this beast, but in any event, it makes not the slightest difference. Given half a chance, the dog's muzzle will bump with startling accuracy into your right testicle, causing you searing pain. The dog then proceeds to run around you, ever more frantic, probably barking, certainly slobbering, examining you for other points of entry.

Now let's make no bones about this: the dog wants to sniff your crotch because it is considering whether or not you are something it can shag. This book is primarily about Grumpy Old Men, but we've all seen parallel experiences happen to women and, even worse, to small children minding their own business on a beach when a bloody great animal puts its paws on their shoulders from behind and anxious parents hurry to the scene.

Now what, I ask you by all that is sacred, is going on here? So far as I can tell, this is unique. We would never put up with a scene like this involving any other creature. Cats don't do it (though, of course, they are irritating for a range of reasons we'll come on to). Why do we put up with this? Why, if some people are going to insist on keeping these horrible animals as household pets, don't we all just carry a big stick when we go for a walk and smack them sharply around the head when they come near?

One of the few redeeming features about dogs, as we know from Pavlov, is that they do learn from their mistakes. (Again, unlike cats. Just think, if Pavlov had kept a cat for a pet instead of a dog, a whole area of psychology would have gone undiscovered.) If dogs received a sharp whack across the nose every time they made an unwelcome advance to a person they have never met before, they might get the picture very quickly. But that's not what happens.

What happens is that, in the rare event that the dog owner has the good grace to apologise, we all say, 'No, don't worry about it, I quite understand.' And that's because, for some reason I can't even begin to fathom, we all seem to want to give the impression that we're dog-lovers. As though that indicated some human quality of which we have a right to be proud.

'No, don't worry, we've got one like it at home.' I've even heard that said by friends I've been walking with who haven't got a dog at home, and when I've pointed this out they reply that they meant that they used to have a dog at home when they were small boys – 35 years ago. As though even that somehow makes them a better person.

Now the reason I tread carefully in this area is that this strange phenomenon can overtake some otherwise reasonably sane and sensible people. One of my best mates, Robert Smallwood, who has provided more than his share of examples for this volume, has the strange brain aberration to which I refer. He's a genuinely good bloke, sane and sensible in all sorts of ways. Hates the Tories, would put a cheese-wire through the neck of Loyd Grossman, a regular stand-up guy.

But when you go to visit his very delightful house in the leafy suburbs of Leeds, where it's always gently drizzling, so the pavements are wet and muddy, you get out of the car to be met by this hysterical, squealing, yapping bag of skin and shit, which you know is immediately going to jump up at you with its muddy paws and ruin the clothes you were thinking of wearing to some smart restaurant later that evening.

Then Robert, and even his lovely wife Amanda – also in other ways a delightful and sensible woman – watch this happening, and gently and patiently suggest to the dog that it shouldn't do that, explaining in carefully enunciated words that 'Uncle Stuart doesn't like dogs'. And they do it with this slightly saddened tone in their voices, which is exactly the one they would use if you were generally a good chap but had allowed your mother to die alone and in agony in a hospital bed without going to visit her. In other words, 'He's a nice enough bloke but he does have this one inexplicable blind spot in his otherwise caring character.'

Now it's true that I don't like dogs, but mostly I just want to be left alone. The thought that I am in some way the 'dog's uncle' provokes in me a very hostile reaction indeed, but let's leave that to one side. The trouble – and I know this must have been spotted and remarked upon elsewhere – is that dogs seem to have a remarkable knack of identifying the one person in a group of a dozen who can't stand them, and then making directly for that person, as though slobbering and drooling all over the new worsted will make them an instant convert. Needless to say, it has the opposite effect on me.

You then brush yourself down, thereby smearing the muddy patches over an even greater surface area of your clothes, and go inside the house. Now Robert and Amanda, it should be said, are about as houseproud a couple as any I know. Their taste in decoration and furniture is sublime. They have scoured the auction houses for fine furniture and pictures, sought out craftsmen to restore original features in the house, paid thousands of pounds for collections of thimbles and porcelain and other knick-knacks, which cover just about every inch of every surface.

The trouble is that their house stinks. It has that stale and fetid stench of somewhere that a pack of hyenas has made its own, but has allowed a couple of humans also to live in for a little while. As you walk in the door, you get an unmistakable lungful of that distinctive smell of dog sweat and dog shit; and that's not the worst thing. No, the worst thing is that when they say how nice it is to see you, would you like a cup of tea, won't you sit down, *you don't actually want to sit down*. I'd rather have my scrotum gently steamed and served in a bamboo basket as a prawn dumpling than sit down. Because the sofa is so covered in dog hairs, and smells so badly of sweaty animal, that you know the stench will transfer instantly to you, and you'll be sniffing it on your own clothes and in your own car for weeks and weeks to come. And thereby you no doubt become an even more irresistible object of desire for the next randy mutt on the beach.

Dogs shit profusely on the pavement, and when their owners still want to drag them along, they shit all across the pavement as well. More conscientious owners walk along with a pocketful of plastic bags and actually grab hold – yes they do – they grab hold of a pile of steaming shit and pop it into a bag for later disposal. We sit and watch dogs methodically licking their arses with no sense of decorum whatsoever, and then immediately go and lick their owners' faces. Faeces then faces.

I rest my case, and excuse me for a moment while I nip out to the bathroom because this has made even me feel nauseous, and I wrote it.

'Uncle Stuart doesn't like dogs'? No he doesn't. He fucking hates them.

Now reading this may come as a shock to lots of dog-owners and dog-lovers, but I'm only writing it for your own good – because your friends love you too much to tell you directly. Just as I love Robert and Amanda far too much to tell them. Now all I have to do is to find a way to stop them from reading this.

Anyway, this rant got in here because half an hour ago we arrived home and next door's dog leapt out suddenly from behind a bush in the pouring rain, thinking it was a sensible idea to attack and destroy the tyres of a moving vehicle. My wife and daughter yelled, 'Stop! Stop!' directly in my ears – I cannot imagine how they got the idea that I might have intended to keep going – and we had to have five minutes of oohing and aahing about how cute he is. Needless to say, when I opened the car door the horrid little runt jumped in, straight on to my lap, thereby instantly depositing about a quarter of a ton of mud and dung on my jeans and pullover. And then, believe it or not, there's a squeal of protest from the family as I shove him off.

That's dogs for you.

Next door's dog

Meanwhile, back at breakfast at home, another thing irritating me is the cats. For some reason that goes back into the distant mists of time to an occasion when we had to compensate my daughter for some misfortune or other, we have two cats, Magic and Muffin. They are brother and sister, the brother bigger than the other, but both have the body-mass of a Christmas turkey you'd buy if the Household Cavalry was spending the festive season with you. And I know for a fact (though I'm not saying how) that neither cat is small enough to fit in the oven.

Now the only thing about cats that I find even vaguely endearing is that they simply don't give a damn. You know the old saying 'There's no such thing as a free lunch'? Well, cats 100 per cent give the lie to that particular piece of homespun wisdom. And, unlike just about every other creature of our experience, human or otherwise, cats don't even try to give the impression that you are going to get something back for your trouble.

Whereas dogs look at you in that pathetic and pleading way, and then want to lick your face or show their gratitude by sniffing your crotch after you've fed them, cats have no interest in raising your hopes. To them, it's clearly your duty and privilege to provide them with whatever is their favourite food of the moment, and they don't give a flying fart about you or anything you care about once they've got what they want. Talk about 'They won't respect you in the morning' – these guys don't respect you in the morning, in the evening, or any time at all.

What they do do is make a horrible mewing racket and do their best to trip you over when they want to be fed, which is most of the time. They assume that you've carefully pasted this particular wallpaper to the walls for their personal use to sharpen their claws. This gives them even greater pleasure if the scratching-post you've bought from the pet shop for this purpose is but a few feet away. They dig their claws into your upholstery, pulling out threads on all your chairs. They rub themselves along the walls, leaving a trail of mud and grease on every corner, and occasionally puke or take a dump on your bedroom carpet.

But no, I tell a lie. It's not quite fair, is it, to suggest that cats never show their appreciation? They do. Occasionally they will carefully disembowel a tiny baby bird that they have wrested from the care of its distraught mother, and place it right in the middle of the kitchen floor to greet you when you come down to breakfast – usually on days when you have a hangover. Intestines over here, remainder of carcass a few feet away. From time to time we've even had larger birds, voles and field mice. And on two occasions Magic and Muffin have designed an ingenious pulley and lever system that has enabled them to drag a pensioned-off and now disfigured squirrel through the cat-flap. Somehow they've also managed to turn it inside out.

Appreciation indeed.

And why do we do it? Why do we put up with it? 'Because they are cute,' I am told, as if this was obvious. Well, I'm afraid I can't see cute. I can't see cute at all. I can see two huge, fat eating machines, which wreck our house, cost us a small fortune in food, vet bills, inoculations, cattery fees and so forth, and don't contribute a thing to my well-being. And yet, god damn it, when they occasionally go missing for a few hours I'm as abject as anyone in the family. And even that makes me grumpy.

So back to breakfast. Where were we? Oh yes, the point is that before I feed myself or anyone else, I have to feed the cats. Once they're fed and off hunting defenceless creatures, we can think about food for humans.

FANCY FOOD

'I can't be doing with all this poncey girl's food; give me baby seal cooked in its own fear. And yet we sort of eat all this and then you start to feel a bit ill and you think, "Oh, I want some salad" ...you know, it's a bit of a macho lie, I think...cos all that hearty comfort food is really nice for a minute, then it's boring. Apart from bacon, eggs and beans, which is really nice.'

JEREMY HARDY

Do you remember those variety packs that contained seven little boxes of different breakfast cereals? Do they still make them? Maybe, but weren't they great when you were a kid? How pathetic must we have been? Just the idea of having a single carton with a measured amount just for you was a kick. The fact that you hated four out of the seven varieties of cereal seemed less important than the apparent extravagance of opening a packet that contained your breakfast portion and nothing else. Snap, crackle, pop. Golden flakes of corn. Although they were already covered with a sticky syrup, you then added loads of milk and sugar, thereby turning a possibly reasonably healthy breakfast into a killer.

Then came muesli. First of all it was bloody Alpen. That was a stroke of genius by the marketing people because if someone had asked me if the British would take to something on the basis that the Swiss liked it, I'd have laughed my head off. Though come to think of it, something like that worked with Toblerone. Have you ever tried eating a big bar of Toblerone? You can't. The peaks of the sodding thing are pushing hard against the roof of your mouth before your teeth can get traction on the valleys, pushing up your top lip alarmingly and making your gums bleed and your eyes water. That's Toblerone. So I wonder how it is that it's one of the few confections that has survived and prospered since my childhood. What happened, I wonder, to 5 Boys? Or Jamboree Bags. Or Black-jacks – four for a penny. Or those squishy prawn-shaped things, lemon quenchers and penny sticks of liquorice? Gone the way of all flesh, but somehow Toblerone survived.

But we were talking about Alpen. We were all persuaded that this mixture of oats and raisins and nuts and honey was the thing to make us look and feel like those very shiny and clear-skinned alpine people. It would probably also improve our yodelling technique. And, oddly enough, if you could stand the friction on your sensitive gums, it didn't taste too bad.

Then someone in our household pointed out that the reason it didn't taste too bad was because there was loads of sugar in it, so suddenly all sorts of varieties of muesli started arriving, in more and more austere packaging, designed to go with our ever more austere dietary regimes. Before we knew where we were we were all eating birdseed mixed up with something that looked like the sweepings from the bottom of the budgie's cage, but tasted worse. Pouring a couple of tablespoonfuls of skimmed or soya 'milk' on it, and using up more calories in grinding through it than it was producing in energy. And having to pretend to like it.

'Not bad,' you'd say over the breakfast table, unsure if you were trying to convince yourself or those around you upon whom you wished the same fate as you were enduring. You'd get halfway through the packet by Wednesday and put the rest out for the birds, vowing to go back to Coco Pops by the weekend.

BATHROOM BLUES

'My band call me Victor Meldrew. My kids call me Victor Meldrew. I actually think that when my hair finally falls out, I'll find that I probably am Victor Meldrew.'

RICK WAKEMAN

I'm usually back upstairs and in the bathroom before anyone else comes down, and getting on with my ablutions. You look in the mirror and what do you see?

I'd like to pause for a moment to share with you my theory about this, and I think if you are in the relevant age range, you'll recognise what I'm describing. As you start to get more advanced in years – 35, 40, 45 – what you see when you look in the mirror is merely an older version of what you remember you looked like when you were 18. That's probably the period in your life when you spent the most time looking in the mirror, so your 18-year-old face is a sort of template for what's coming next. Now when you look you see that person, that basic face, but with the added lines, sagging jaw and greying hair sort of superimposed. You are seeing an 18-year-old with the stage make-up of a middle-aged man.

Meanwhile, the rest of the world – most of which has no idea what you looked like when you were an 18-year-old Adonis – are just seeing an old git. They don't have that subconscious reference point that you have, so they're just seeing a grey, late middle-aged old sod, who's well on his way to the grave. There may even be a period where you're deluding yourself that you're wearing quite well for your years. 'A reasonably attractive older man,' you might think. Forget it. You're invisible at best, offensive at worst.

Recently, caught out in the rain, I briefly and, as it turned out, unwisely put on one of those beany hats belonging to my daughter. While I'm imagining myself a slightly older and more distinguished version of Enrique Iglesias, the rest of the world is seeing Compo.

Then finally the day arrives, and it's probably one morning after a particularly heavy night, when you look in the mirror

and you get a shock. Looking back at you is a complete stranger. Suddenly you realise that the face reflected in the mirror is nothing at all like the face you remember aged 18. No longer that same young face but with added lines and wrinkles and sagging jaw-line. Indeed, someone else seeing you now, and seeing a photograph of you aged 18, might well have difficulty realising that it was the same person. You've become someone else. You've become your own father.

This adds to your grumpiness and further exacerbates the problem because the diagonal lines that have developed on my forehead from continual frowning have become so intermeshed with the horizontal lines that are a symptom of my constant amazement at the stupidity of the world around me that people could now play bloody noughts and crosses on the expanding space below my hairline.

Back in the bathroom, I've brushed my teeth and flossed my gums because every time I go to the dentist I have to endure the hygienist talking to me like I'm a 12-year-old. Worse yet, when her various implements of destruction are in my mouth I feel like a 12-year-old. And that's another thing my parents never had to put up with. Sure, their teeth rotted and fell out, but at least they didn't have to submit to being ticked off by a slip of a girl half their age.

But now it's time to hop into the bath. Bathtime used to be fun – even the quick 'in and out' I usually have in the morning. I don't mean ducks or boats or anything; what on earth do you take me for? No, I used to like to luxuriate for a few minutes and just enjoy the feeling of immersion. A chance to contemplate some of the forbidden things there ought to be a law against, and indeed in some territories there probably is. Nowadays, of course, a bath isn't just a bath; it's an opportunity for another of the tyrannies we grumpies are subject to: yes, it's 'self-examination'.

LOOKING FOR TROUBLE

'So I looked in the mirror and there it was, this black spot, plainly a melanoma... I mean, no doubt about it. Best thing to do? Nothing. Go to the doctor, he's going to say, "Go to the hospital, do a biopsy." Comes back, yes, it's cancer. You're history and you die. Or don't go the doctor, get cancer and die. Saves you going to the hospital.'

JEREMY CLARKSON

I reckon that if someone had suggested to my father that he should fondle his own bollocks while in the bath, he would have punched them on the nose. Not in his latter years, of course, when he was a bit more sensible, but as a younger man. 'What do you take me for?' he would have said, 'some sort of a poofter?' He mellowed eventually, my dad, but he was what, in those days, they used to call 'a man's man'. And those were the days when self-abuse made you blind.

Nowadays we not only have to be in touch with our feminine side, of which no doubt more later, but also more in touch with our own bodies. Literally. We have to take the opportunity for the warm water to have made our scrotums nice and pliable, and have a careful feel around to try to identify unfamiliar lumps and bumps.

Now I don't really want to do this, and I certainly don't want to be caught doing it. And one reason why I don't like doing it is that I don't think I've ever done it and not thought something might be a bit odd. What the hell is normal anyway? Is that a bump or a tube? On one occasion I'd been doing quite a lot of cycling and felt a touch tender in that area, and decided to go to see my GP – like we're all supposed to these days. No embarrassment, just modern man stuff.

Being a sensible chap, and anyway certainly not wanting to be the person who tells me not to worry only to find my left testicle blows up to the size and shape of a Rubik's cube, my GP sent me off to the hospital for further examination. Quickly. This is one of those rare occasions that you can get a follow-up appointment in the same decade as the referral.

This is not a picnic. I try hard, no I really do, to take all these things in my stride. Nothing to be embarrassed about. It's all just routine and medical. They've all seen it a thousand times before. But put your hand on your heart, if you're a bloke, and tell me that when you go for one of these examinations you aren't worried that it's looking a bit sheepish. A wee bit under par. And the only thing that could possibly be worse is if, for some reason, it's looking a bit over-excited. Anyway, I won't dwell on it because it's not clever and it's not

funny; the important thing is that they told me everything was normal, but that I was right to bring it to their attention and at my age it would be as well to self-examine regularly.

I wonder if this is really right. A GP friend of mine told me recently that he is absolutely sick to the back teeth of neurotic menopausal men coming in and saying they think they might have a lump 'down there'. He has to take it seriously, just as my GP had to take mine seriously, but he hasn't had a confirmed case of a real problem in years.

In the end, I suppose that fingering your bollocks in the bath or shower isn't the end of the world, but, being a grumpy old sod, I worry about where it will all lead. When are we going to be asked to examine our own prostates? How long before we're given a spatula or camera on a string and asked to give our bowels a quick check-up? Yes, I know you're saying it's unthinkable now, but that's what my dad would have said about fiddling with his testicles. It's only a question of time, you mark my words.

HIDING A MULTITUDE

'I just dress in what is comfortable and covers up my gut as much as possible, because the problem is that I look like a mini-cab driver. You know there are some of us that are just fated to look like a mini-cab driver. It doesn't matter what clothes you put on, or how much you pay for them, you're still going to look like a mini-cab driver.'

JOHN PEEL

For many years I was something of a suit in the television industry, and had a selection of about a dozen of them hanging in the wardrobe. They came mostly from Jaeger or Aquascutum, and ran the whole spectrum of colour from dark grey via navy blue to black, and from double-breasted to single-breasted. One or two even had a faintly discernible pinstripe. Yes, I was a byword throughout the business for being a pioneer of fashion.

No, really, my taste in suits was always dull and boring and, yes, I always felt like a small boy dressing up in my dad's clothes. But the main virtue of this strange uniform was that it absolved me of a whole set of decisions that the real Grumpy Old Man struggles with. What the devil to wear.

This was not a problem for our parents. At the age of 21 our dads started dressing like their dads, and never wavered from that for the whole of their lives. You've seen pictures of them, many times, as younger men. Conservative suit and stiff white collar. For holidays or relaxing, a pair of cavalry twill trousers, some light grey flannels perhaps, and a sports jacket. Towards the last years of his life, my own father used to wear slightly more relaxed clothes, but I don't believe I ever saw him go out for the evening without wearing a tie, and I know for a fact that he never wore a T-shirt or a sweatshirt in his whole life.

Going back one generation further, to my grandfather, everyone was even more buttoned up. Like me, you've probably got one or more of those sepia photos of the whole family, in which they all sit in a very formal pose in a photographer's studio. Mum and Dad sitting in chairs, with their brood arranged tidily around them, and a potted aspidistra growing out of their heads. All of them, in their Sunday best, have very neatly brushed hair, none of them smiling.

We have just such a photo in which, I can work out by the date, my grandfather must be aged 21. He looks like today's 41. His hair is receding, and is greased and swept back to give maximum emphasis to the fact. He wears a pinstriped suit and a shirt with a detachable starched collar – a uniform that he went on to wear every day for the rest of his life. Yes, I mean every day. Though he's barely shaving at the time this picture was taken, within the next two years he is sporting a full moustache, just like his own father. In fact he could easily be mistaken for his own father, and probably was.

When these guys opened the wardrobe door, they had a choice of the dark grey winter worsted or the slightly paler grey summer worsted. That was it. Grandad used to do his gardening in his suit. No kidding.

Now this may sound eccentric and a bit inhibiting, but it did have the virtue of saving them from too much choice. Choosing what to wear just wasn't an issue. They all looked like their dads and they all looked like each other.

Today's Grumpy Old Man has the opposite problem and simply does not know what to wear. You don't want to look like your dad, and the only thing you want less than that is to look like your kids.

I've got one friend, William, who is now 52 and dresses like an 18-year-old. The latest trainers, with luminescent flashes and unpronounceable names on the sides – Nike, Adibadas. The latest style of parachute pants or designer jeans. The latest labels in T-shirts and sweatshirts. He even wore those strange Puffa jackets when they were in fashion. His clothes have zips and Velcro in all sorts of unexpected places. His trousers have all sorts of pockets in them, some of them unusable. He has bomber jackets and leather jackets, and a vast collection of trainers that look as though they were designed for moon-walking. One pair – suspend your usual powers of credulity for a moment – one pair has a light on the heel that flashes as he walks.

Have you ever heard of anything so preposterous?

Now because I've known William for years and years, this eccentricity has become his trademark and suits his engaging character. At least he has the good grace to laugh at himself.

But I do think that this behaviour is halfway to certifiable. Someone told me the other day that, when it refers to women, this phenomenon is called 'Kronenberg' after 'Kronenberg 1669'. In other words, they look 16 from the back and when they turn around they look 69. I'd rather join the Hare Krishna movement and shuffle down the high street chanting and ringing finger tambourines than go out in the street dressed like he does. What could possibly be more ridiculous than some daft old dandy pretending to be a teenager?

So I don't want to dress younger than I am. On the other hand, I don't want to dress like my dad. Richard Madeley complained vehemently about this in the TV series: he'd been leaving his house when he was snapped by a photographer from the *Evening Standard*. He was wearing a pair of jeans, ordinary trainers, a leather jacket, had a bag over his shoulder and was riding a bike. The caption on the article said 'Welcome to the world of Muttonman'. 'What am I supposed to wear?' said Richard rather plaintively. 'An old mac and a flat cap, with bicycle clips like my dad?' I thought he had a point when I heard him say that, but made a mental note to stop wearing my bicycle clips.

So what, indeed, are we to do? Wear what our dads wore, or the alternative, which seems to involve paying ridiculous sums of money for more comfortable clothes that have all those lunatic designer labels on the outside?

We Grumpy Old Men can't get our heads around this. At one time labels were things that went on the inside, and were a bloody nuisance if they popped out. Rory McGrath claims to ask the people in GAP if they can cut off the label, or give him a discount for promoting their products. They look at him as though he's potty, and maybe he is – after all, he bursts into three rousing choruses of 'Tie a Yellow Ribbon round the Old Oak Tree' if the person next to him on the train starts using a mobile phone. But, barking or not, why should he be a walking billboard for a multinational clothes business?

And apart from baulking at wearing the equivalent of a sandwich board, we also object to the ludicrous difference in price of this reasonably OK plain grey sweatshirt, and this reasonably OK plain grey sweatshirt with 'Timberland' written on it. Most of the time we just won't go there, and if we have, it's usually under duress, or it's been a gift.

So what do we end up with? We don't want to wear designer labels, and we don't want to wear old git stuff. So we end up with one of those sub-designer, mass-produced but not quite total rubbish things like 'Blue Harbour' from Marks & Spencer. Now what could possibly be sadder than that? What could possibly be sadder?

This is one of those things, for me, like finding yourself shouting at *Top of the Pops* or tut-tutting when you see someone who has tattooed the top of their shaved head. Shopping in Marks & Spencer: a sure sign that it's all over. You find yourself browsing along the racks and railings, desperately trying to find something you don't actually hate. You glance up and all around you are a load of totally boring old bastards, who look as though they have had their spirits ripped out of them with white-hot tongs, almost always out shopping with their wives. He's looking bored, depressed, repressed and generally hopeless, while she's rifling through a whole load of stripy rugby shirts to try to find one that will make him look even more fat-headed than he does now. Underneath his anorak. And then it all gets worse because you think, 'Oh, my God, that's how I look!' – and at this stage I hightail it out of the shop as fast as my fat little legs will carry me.

So where to go? I can just about stand to go into GAP, but if I suddenly find myself surrounded by teenagers, I feel a cold sweat creeping over me and can't get out fast enough. Top

Shop? Dunno, wouldn't ever dream of going in. Burtons? Do they still exist? Anyway, too boring. I find that the answer is to go into one of those big departments stores, such as Bentalls, where they have all the different ranges, so that if you accidentally stray into something too young for you, you can beat a retreat without too much indignity. You can toy with the idea of buying something by Kenzo or Jasper Conran, without making the commitment of going into a dedicated store. And, of course, you would never actually go ahead and buy any of these designers – have you seen their bloody prices?

One little problem that I have is that I will only ever wear grey, black or very muted shades of blue. So I've got literally dozens of tiny variations on the theme. But then, just now and again, I find myself in somewhere like Austin Reed, wondering if I should ring the changes with this rugby shirt in maroon with a wide black hoop round it.

As I am about to reconcile myself with what, for me, is the equivalent of coming out as gay, I discover that it's got the number 12 written on the back. I return it to the shelf as though I've just been given an electric shock. The idea of walking around with a number on my back, or on my left tit, as though I were some kind of pensioned-off sportsmen seems so preposterous to me that I can hardly breathe when I think about it. Don't you think it's a great laugh that the only people wearing sportsmen's tracksuits in the high street are 30 stone? What is going on in their heads? Are we supposed to think they are Olympic champions in pie-eating, or off-duty sumo wrestlers?

Eventually I find myself back in Marks & Spencer, where I finally settle for yet another black sweatshirt, with the slight concession that this one has a white collar. It may also have that little tag on one side with the red flag or whatever it is on it, but at least I know I can cut that off when I get home. Blue Harbour? Fuck right off.

Anyway, right about now I'm ready to go to work and I leave the house and get in the car.

WHEEL US OUT, SCOTTIE

'The reason we drive motor cars is that once we've got one, we're free. But the conflict between that idealism and the reality that you get in your motor car is that you're exposed, not to freedom, opportunities, discovery, delight — you're exposed to frustration, dirt, danger and aggression, and that's what makes us so cross. That, I believe, is the source of road rage.' STEPHEN BAYLEY

The car opens up a whole new world of irritations for me, and for just about every Grumpy Old Man I know. But before we get to them, let's talk about some of the good things about the car, which account for the fact that it's the object of the greatest love affair of the 20th and 21st centuries. On the plus side, the car is one of the few bits of space that we can more or less call our own. We can sit quietly in a reasonably comfortable seat for the half hour before we get to the next set of traffic lights, and generally have a bit of time for contemplation. Especially if we don't need to arrive at our destinations any time in the next three days.

Car designers, you have to hand it to them, have got us big daft lads worked out pretty well. We like dials on the dashboard that look as though they were originally designed to be in a plane, perhaps a Spitfire, with an old-fashioned pointer and traditional numbers on the speedo. And then sometimes on a Harrier jump-jet, with loads of digital read-outs. I recently had a car that told me the speed, the engine revs, my average speed over the journey, the temperature inside, the temperature outside, the day and date, the number of miles I could drive until I ran out of petrol and, yes, believe it or not, the height above sea-level. I asked the dealer if anyone had ever used this startling facility, and he said that he had one customer who was a hot-air balloonist.

John Peel was very funny about this in the TV series. With disarming honesty, he confessed that there were several controls in his current car that he hasn't actually touched because he doesn't know what they do. However, the car seems to go all right without him knowing, so he hasn't worried about it. We probed this a little further, and it turns out that he's referring to the cruise control.

John was also irritated to find that his enjoyment of music on the radio is constantly interrupted by someone telling him the traffic conditions on the M25. His journey home doesn't actually take him on the M25, and even if it did, he wouldn't have taken enough notice of the exit numbers for the information to be of any use. The trouble is that he doesn't know how to turn this facility off. Here is John Peel, who has been in radio since God was a small boy, who must have done more radio self-operation than almost anyone alive, and he doesn't know how to turn off the traffic information. Truly the genuine article. (Just for John – you press the button marked TA.)

This is only the most vivid example of a syndrome we all suffer from. We like toys, even if we don't know how to use them and don't want to use them. My latest car, a VW Polo, has a devilishly ingenious device on the dashboard which springs out to hold a cup or can. Cup-holders are, I am reliably informed, a must these days in all cars. Occasionally, when bored, I press the device that springs the cup-holder out and then push it back in again, just to marvel at the wondrous design. However, I've had the car for a year and have never yet had occasion to put a cup or can in the cup-holder. I've tried to put my phone in it once or twice, only to have it fall out, but never a cup. No, never a cup.

So cars are a fascinating environment in which to study the mores of the Grumpy Old Man. Next time you are in a traffic jam take the opportunity to look closely at the faces of the people driving cars in the other direction. You will undoubtedly find them wearing a range of different expressions, from the fairly bland to the about-to-explode. But if they are Grumpy Old Men – anywhere between 35 and 54 – you can be sure that behind that apparently ordinary exterior they will be in turmoil. They look like ordinary geezers just going about their business, but it's all going on inside.

The eyes float languidly across to the bloke in the bright yellow VW, apparently quite passive, but behind them the brain is ticking over. 'Look at that prat. Doesn't he realise that the new Beetle is a girl's car? What does he think he looks like? He's probably got a plastic flower on the dashboard.' To the casual observer he might seem totally at ease as he edges up too close to the Porsche in front, but all the while the mind is gently churning: 'Nice car, the Boxster, but if I could afford a Porsche, I'd get a proper one. And anyway, someone ought to tell that bloke that the combination of pony-tail and bald patch is not a good look.' Or, waiting apparently calmly at the traffic lights, he's actually thinking, 'Great, no one crossing the road and no pedestrians as far as the eye can see, and we're all sitting like bloody idiots here while the light stays red for a quarter of a century.' And other assorted pleasantries.

Imagine the debate that must have gone on when the idea of traffic lights was first thought of. 'This won't work,' someone would have said, 'because nobody is going to sit there in their cars, waiting for a red light to change, when it's as clear as it could possibly be that there is nothing coming the other way. People just won't do it. We're British, for heaven's sake, not bloody Japanese.' Well, they were wrong, weren't they? We are Japanese after all.

I used to play this game when I was in Tokyo a few years ago. How to kill 200 Japanese in one go. You'd be standing on the pavement, waiting to cross the road, and the little red man would be illuminated. Hundreds of people are waiting to cross the road. As far as the eye can see, in any direction, there are no cars. You step off the pavement and start to walk. At that moment, the people who have not been looking at the red light, see you step off the pavement, assume the red light has changed and start to walk with you. Scores of them start to cross. Then a few of them look up and see that the red man is still illuminated, and go quickly into reverse. Meanwhile, the people behind them are still walking. It's carnage.

Back in Britain, you see this phenomenon at its most stark when you come across road works on a country lane or in the middle of nowhere. You can see the road ahead right up to the horizon two miles away. There are no cars in sight. There are no pedestrians or the possibility of them. No junction from which a car could suddenly appear. Yet the traffic light is on red, and there are Sidney and Doreen sitting in their Austin Maestro in front of you waiting for it to change to green.

I always drive around them, but can feel Sidney and Doreen's eyes boring into the back of my head. And can you imagine the conversation with the policeman? 'You went through the red light.' 'I know, but I could see that there was nothing coming.' 'That's not the point. Suppose everyone did that?' 'If everyone went through the red light when it was perfectly clear that there was nothing coming, I don't think it would matter.' 'Oh, a wise-arse, eh? You're nicked.'

So as we're sitting in our cars, we're watching the world around us, and just about everything we see pisses us off in some way or another. Billboards with varieties of FCUK on them, or advertising stuff that is obviously not intended for us because we don't know what it is. We're looking around at the idiots with every square inch of their bodies pierced so that all you want to do is grab a stray eyelet and yank hard. The louts wearing parkas with hoods turned up and riding BMXs whom you'd like to strafe. The girls wearing cutaway tops that don't cover their stomachs when, boy, you really don't want to see their stomachs. BMW drivers – it's always BMW drivers – who are impatient that you haven't immediately driven forward to fill the three-inch gap between you and the car in front, and who either give you a blast on the twin-tone horn they had installed as a Christmas present from Sharon, or squeal around you to edge into the space.

Worse than that, even worse, and in fact I think this is the very worst thing of all: drivers who take advantage of the fact that you've pulled over to let an ambulance go by to try to get past you. This must have happened to you. You've pulled up at the kerb, or on the kerb, to let the ambulance or fire engine past, and there is an arsehole in a BMW right behind him trying to jump the queue of traffic. This is definitely one to make you reach for the Kalashnikov. My mate Alan thinks it is demonstrable by scientific analysis that BMW drivers actually have lower IQs than the average. He's suggesting that we do a test. Mind you, Alan is more than averagely grumpy; and anyway, who's he to talk – he's just bought a Mini Cooper.

You see a lot of those 'neither nowt nor summat' cars on the roads – like Accords or Preludes, that sort of stuff. Neither totally cool nor totally crap – sort of the 'Blue Harbour' of motor vehicles. I can understand why you might see old and used cars like these, because if you don't have a lot of money to spend on a car and anyway you don't care much about them, you maybe just want four wheels and will take whatever you can get second-hand. What I can't understand is being able to spend all that money to buy a new car, and then choosing a Datsun Sunny. Why would anybody want to do that? You can choose any car from a selection of about a thousand costing £9000 and you choose a Honda Praline. Or a Ford Pretzel or something. It's not so much that these cars are badly designed, it's more that they aren't designed at all. They're not even cars really; they're more just a heap of junk on four reasonably well-engineered tyres. They're a eurobox. Do you remember the Austin Allegro? How could anyone have had a choice of any other car, any car from dozens, and still have chosen an Austin Allegro?

And here's another thing. You are buying a car new and can have any colour you like, and you choose a red one. You have your choice of all sorts of shades of blue – pale, dark, navy, sky and so on; you can have black, you can have white, there's a quite nice British racing green, and you make an actual positive decision to buy a red one. What is this telling us about you? Well, maybe it's just me, but it's telling me that you're a dickhead.

There's only one car in history that looks good in red, and that's a Ford Mustang. If you have the opportunity to drive along Route 1 between San Francisco and Los Angeles, then buy a load of Beach Boys CDs and get yourself a red Ford Mustang. Other than that, what message are you trying to send us by choosing red as the colour of your brand new car? Boy racer? Toss-pot? Well, it worked.

And how about 4 x 4s? I don't want to say a lot about this because we'll be going on about them when we come to talk about the school run a bit later, and, anyway, I used to have one. Well, actually I had one after another. But honestly, it is totally preposterous, isn't it? Will Self especially detests the ones with bull-bars – taking little Chloe and Tarquin to school up the Fulham High Road and mowing down any other child who might get in the way. 'Don't drive it down the high street,' says Will, 'go on the Pamplona bull-run.' 'I need it for the hills,' you hear the owners say. 'No, you don't,' says John Sessions, 'you need it to make your penis look bigger.' Case closed.

I read that 4 x 4s, or what the Americans call SUVs (sports utility vehicles), now account for fully half of the US automobile market. I remember hearing the American comedienne Roseanne Barr talking about how her by then estranged husband insisted on driving one of those para-military Humvees around Los Angeles. 'You might run over a landmine on Sunset Strip,' she reflected, 'you might…'

Every time you drive anywhere on a route you haven't driven for a few weeks, someone has thought up an ever more ingenious way of making your journey more difficult. It might be that you can no longer turn right where you used to turn right, and all the right turns from here to Canterbury are blocked off – and it's now clear you had to turn left 100 yards further back and then right and right again. Too late now, though, because there are no U-turns.

It might be that someone has decided to narrow the road at a particular point to one lane and to give the right of way to the traffic coming against you, so there's a queue of cars from here to Dusseldorf waiting for a solitary milk-float with a fatter and even less endearing version of Benny Hill at the wheel to glide by – whistling 'Ernie'.

It might be that someone has decided that what this road needs is a new series of sleeping policemen to guard against the unlikely event that the traffic can go more than 10 miles per hour. And for added amusement, it might be that they have positioned these obstructions so that drivers can put one tyre either side of them, but only by swerving dangerously into the middle of the road, and thereby encountering the poor sods coming the other way and trying to do the same thing.

And who was it who said all this was OK? Where did the local politicians and local government officers and aldermen or whatever they are called get the impression that it was OK to put all these obstacles in our way as we try to go about our general everyday business? We take all this stuff for granted, grumble about it, but do we ever wonder how this stuff is allowed?

Sure, presumably these cretins were elected to their positions by about one in ten of those eligible to vote. But where in their mandate did it say they could spend our hard-earned money making our lives more difficult? Nowhere, that's bloody where. They just decided to do it. They went to their stupid meetings, in their ridiculous little council chambers, drank their tea and ate their Fruesli bars, then made themselves feel even more important by being elected by their new mates to a position on the Highways Committee.

Then, and this really defines the expression 'adding insult to injury', if you live outside an arbitrary boundary in London determined by Bloody Ken Sodding Livingstone – yes, that is in fact his full and proper name and title – you are forced to pay an extra £5 a day for the privilege of putting up with this totally preposterous shit. £5 a day for the so-called 'congestion charge'. £25 a working week, £100 a month, £1200 a year. And this is after-tax money, so you have to have earned about £1700 on top of all the other expenses involved in running a car – buying it, road tax, insurance, MOT and petrol – just to get to work, to earn the money, to pay the taxes, to fund the little local busybodies who sit round in committee rooms over cups of cold tea and dream up new ways to make our lives a misery. These guys must be having a laugh.

And if you don't live in or near London, you may be sitting there feeling smug at the moment, but be assured that this execrable crapulence is coming your way very soon. Half of the preposterous prats who supposedly run our towns and cities up and down Britain are watching and waiting for the chance of the same power trip that this latest piece of oppression gave Ken.

Oh, and has it eased congestion in London? Of course it hasn't. It did for a few weeks, but now it's back to the normal gridlock. When the congestion charge was introduced they said it would be withdrawn 'if it didn't work'. Fat chance, because guess who gets to decide if it works or not? Yes, you got it, the same people who introduced it in the first place. And guess who votes for them? Yes, that's right, people living inside London, and not paying the congestion charge, who are only too happy to see other people pay to drive past their houses. Well, I told you not to get me started.

So, where were we? Oh yes, in our cars and on the way to work.

HARPING ON ABOUT HEALTH

'I am trying to diet at the moment, and what I've suddenly realised is that all you need to do is to pick up food and feel how heavy it is. If you pick up a piece of meat it's heavy, right? You pick up some vegetables, they're light. OK? You put vegetables in your body, they ain't going to make you heavy. You put meat in your body, it is. End of story as far as I'm concerned.'

RICK STEIN

One of the things that is sent to amuse all of us who have the regular pleasure of sitting in our vehicles and smelling the clutch burn out is watching cyclists and runners travelling so much faster than we are. I'm always impressed to see people running to work, with a kit-bag on their backs, obviously carrying the clothes they are going to change into. I used to wonder how all these people happened to work for companies that were kind enough to make showering facilities available to their staff. Then I had occasion once to visit County Hall and to sit close to someone who had run to work, and realised that maybe I had been naive.

Still, running to work seems a sensible idea. If the journey is less than 6 miles through a built-up area, it's probably quicker than driving. It's true that you have a very good chance of being run over by a car or motorcycle, you get to inhale all those vehicle fumes deep into your lungs, you wreck your knee joints on hard pavements, you sweat for most of the morning, wear crumpled-up clothes all day and then slip on the ice on your way home and spend the evening in A & E. However, all that's better than driving.

Cycling feels like much the same: you get all of the above – plenty of sweat and danger – but with the added benefits of being able to wear a ridiculous helmet and moist Lycra, while risking a mild case of erectile dysfunction after long hours of sitting in the saddle.

No, exercise in general is the bane of the lives of the modern Grumpy Old Man. Be honest – did your dad ever take any exercise? Of course he didn't. Did his dad? Certainly not. The reason is that they probably had to work for a living, and therefore hadn't the necessity, the energy or the time to do anything else when they got home.

We, by contrast, are absolutely persecuted by it from dawn to dusk. It's everywhere we look. Every second item on the news is about obesity. Every third item is about a new killer disease or a new take on an old killer disease. Every fourth item is about how a food that we spent all our lives thinking was good for us has now been found to be bad for us.

We all grew up in those post-war, post-rationing years being told by our parents to drink the full-fat milk and eat as many eggs as we could get down because it was good for us. They really thought they were doing us a favour. Now we find that all the time we were storing up little fat cells, and these little fat cells that we nurtured so lovingly never go away. Sure, if we watch our diet and run around like lunatics all our lives, they'll stay sleepy and quiescent. But they are always waiting for the first bloody big plate of chips or three pints of lager, and then they expand again to turn you with alarming speed from lean young hunter into the Pilsbury Dough-boy.

Hence the life-sentence we're all condemned to of fighting obesity. Galloping lardiness is overtaking smoking as the biggest self-inflicted killer. The item on the TV news is illustrated by shots of great fat wobble-bottoms gallumping down the streets, huge midriffs bulging over jeans and enormous breasts protruding from too-tight T-shirts. Yes, yes, I know, you can see it coming – the women are no better either.

I sometimes find myself wondering how you'd feel if you were to recognise yourself in one of those shots. The camera person always discreetly cuts off the heads of the people he or she has alighted on to illustrate the lard item – but if it were you, I think you'd know it. The shots of women from the back are the best. Often they seem to have quite a slim waist, but have decided to wear a very tight pair of jeans, which has the effect of giving them a huge arse. They have probably asked their partner, 'Does my bum look big in these?' and being a sensible soul who just wants a quiet life, he replied, 'Not at all dear, you look great.' And all the time he's thinking, 'Oh, my God, what a fright.'

But what if you're someone who has managed to kid yourself that you're not in bad shape? Sure, you're not the stick-thin, eat-what-you-like lad of 20 that you once were, but, all things considered, you're in fairly good nick. Then you see yourself illustrating a news item about rhino smugglers. That silhouette of the Michelin man is in fact you. That wouldn't exactly make your day, now would it?

So we've all got to watch what we eat, and turn up twice a week at the local gym for a bit of ritual humiliation, maybe under the watchful eye of a personal trainer. Now this is a real modern phenomenon. Personal trainers. These are people to whom you pay £50 an hour to humiliate you, just because you

haven't got the will-power to do it on your own. You can do this in a gymnasium, or you can walk into any London telephone box and find a postcard advertising a dominatrix, and she'll humiliate you for about the same price. You are paying this person to make you suffer. I would personally lose so many calories through the stress of knowing I was this stupid, and that a hyper-muscled airhead was fleecing me so blatantly, that I wouldn't need to exercise at all.

Tony Hawks said that he used to turn up at the gym and find himself running on a machine alongside 20 other people watching MTV. It suddenly occurred to him that running round the park was healthier, more interesting and free, so that's what he does now. But don't come crying to me when you're whammed in the *cojones* by the nose of an amorous bull-terrier.

I saw an interview the other day with the wonderful lawyer and writer John Mortimer, during which he recounted that his doctor had asked him if he got out of breath when taking exercise. Mortimer had looked at him quizzically, genuinely, I think, failing to understand the question. 'How would I know?' he asked. He went on to recommend a succession of small illnesses as a way to avoid being persuaded to exert oneself, and, if necessary, to invent an injury and refer to 'my old trouble'. In the same programme Tony Benn quoted an old cleric who'd said that if the urge to take exercise came upon you, he recommended that you should lie down until the feeling passed. That had been Tony Benn's practice. He'd also smoked a pipe and drunk thousands of gallons of tea over half a century and at 79 was still running around the country on a schedule that would tax a 19-year-old.

By contrast, I always think of that American runner called Jim Fixx, who claimed to have started the international mania for jogging. Maybe he did. He wrote a book about how he'd been an overweight journalist who drank and smoked and was on his way to an early grave. His dad had died young, so he was especially determined to stay fit and live long. Jim Fixx keeled over and died aged 53 while out running.

So I say bollocks to the gymnasium, bollocks to healthy eating, I merely say fie to personal trainers (because I happen to know one or two), and certainly bollocks to fashionable diets. None of it works: it's all in your genes. If your dad died young, you're going to as well; and if he lived to 95, you will too – unless you get mown down by a 4 x 4 with a bull-bar or run over by a tour bus full of Americans tourists wearing shorts.

SIGNS OF THE TIMES

'A bulldozer is the only answer to London's street furniture. There's no good protesting. In fact, if you protested, you'd probably have to have a meeting, and they'd put up signs to say that a meeting was taking place. No, a bulldozer, straight down the middle.'

MATTHEW PARRIS

So you stop for a newspaper and some cigarettes or sweeties. Everyone needs sustenance in the hour that a 6-mile journey is going to take, but where are you going to park?

Well, not on the street because someone we didn't bother to go out and vote against on polling day has decided to make our lives as difficult as possible, and our streets as ugly as possible, by painting lines everywhere. Just stand back sometime and take an objective look at the average city street. It's all happened so gradually, over such a long period, that we kind of take it for granted and don't really see. But if you do take the trouble to look around you, it's as if someone has tried to turn our environment into a piece of hostile art; the urban design equivalent of Munch's *The Scream*.

These guys have painted double lines in bright yellow along the gutter to tell you that you can't park. Then they've painted a double yellow flash across the edge of the kerb, just in case you can't see the double yellow lines in the gutter. Sometimes they've painted a single yellow line, and then you've got to look for a notice that tells you the nature of the parking restriction, and usually it's 'at any time'. Does this mean you can park at any time, in which case why do we need the yellow line? Or does it mean you can't park at any time, in which case why is it a single and not a double yellow line? Elsewhere it says 'Residents' Parking' or 'Pay at Meter 4–7 a.m., 4–10 p.m.' I guess this means you can park if you have a resident's parking permit, but if not, you have to pay. But do you have to pay within the times mentioned, or outside them?

Sometimes it's not a double yellow line but a double red line, which I understand means that it's a red route, where you cannot park at all. So that's clear. Don't park; but how is that different from a double yellow line?

They have put meters all along the edge of the street, which make parking so expensive that if you stand there feeding them with 20-pence pieces, the bought time expires faster than you can insert the coins. Sometimes, just for fun, they'll put the parking meter right at the line dividing one bay from another, and you don't know which meter to put your money into. Yes, that's happened to me: I put about £12 in the meter for an hour and a half stay, and came back to find a parking ticket. I'd put the money in the wrong meter. This kind of situation illustrates the wisdom of rigorous gun control. If at that moment I'd had an AK47, I probably would have wiped out half the traffic wardens in south London.

If it weren't enough that they've erected traffic islands in the middle of the roads, they have also started putting little islands jutting out from the side of the roads, which are supposed to have the effect of slowing everyone down. Unfortunately, what they also do is to compel cyclists to swerve out into the traffic, thereby rendering themselves prey to idiot motorists who are driving while sending texts to their girlfriends. And when the drivers swerve into the middle of the road to avoid the obstacle and/or the cyclist, they happily nudge the motorcyclist they haven't seen on their near side into the path of an approaching double-decker. Good thinking, chaps.

They put up signs telling us of cycle lanes, one-way streets, culs-de-sac and no through roads; children crossing, pedestrian crossings and cross old people crossing; signs that seem to indicate a man having trouble with an umbrella. There are signs telling us of a weak bridge ahead. What are we supposed to do, tiptoe? Signs telling us of low-flying aircraft – what are we supposed to do, duck? Signs on the motorway telling us to avoid running deer. When did you last see a deer on a motorway, and what would you do differently having seen the sign? My favourite one of all, my very favourite, is the sign that indicates that huge rocks and boulders are likely to come tumbling down into the road ahead from the vast cliff-face alongside you and overhanging the carriageway. Now I don't know about you, but whenever I see that I close the sunroof.

Motorway driving is a whole additional thrill. Most vindictive are the signs above the M25 that warn you not to drive above 40. Who among us has seen that sign and not said, out loud, 'Oh, for the joy of being able to drive as fast as 40.' There are signs warning us of road works 1 mile ahead lasting from May this year to September next, and if you are still awake 45 minutes later when you eventually reach the road works, you can be sure there will be no one working. Instead there will be miles and miles and miles of traffic cones, closing off one lane with no obstruction in it except maybe a pile of gravel at the beginning and another at the end. Now and again there may be the odd bulldozer or Portaloo for added plausibility, but that's optional. If you are still awake after all this queuing, there is the occasional reminder that 'Tiredness Kills'. Let's leave out the smart-mouth remarks and simply observe that 'it doesn't'.

ROAD TO RUIN

'I tell you what, at times I think I should never have been a musician, I should have been a cone-maker. I mean, nobody knew what the cones hotline was in the first place, and when you phoned, you said, "I've *spotted some cones." "How many?" "About four and a half million on the M6, doing absolutely nothing." "Thank you for telling us." It's amazing, isn't it?'*

RICK WAKEMAN

If it becomes totally impossible to park on the street, you could always go to a shopping centre and park in the multi-storey. We'll leave to one side the limited height restrictions and occasional joy of seeing someone who's forgotten that they haven't taken off the roof-rack or, better still, have a bike on the roof. I've seen that only once and it is amazing how much mess it can make.

Now I'm not going to go into a lot of detail about multi-storeys, partly because Bill Bryson had great fun with it in *Notes*

from a Small Island, but I do wonder if there can be a more catastrophic example of British design than these awful monstrosities.

Of course they have to optimise the use of space, but what is the point of designing the turning circle between ramps so that cars over 6 feet long have to do a three-point turn to negotiate them? Of course they have to have plenty of pillars in the structure, but what is the point of positioning a parking bay right next to them so you can't get out of the driver's door? Of course they have to decide the average car width and mark out bays efficiently, but as soon as one idiot parks a few inches away from the centre of his bay, the next car is nudged to one side, and the bay you have to edge into is 6 inches narrower than it should be. You can just about squeeze the car into the bay, but then you can't get out of the door. So you sit and ponder.

Could you drive forward, get out of the car, and push the car back into the space? Probably not, it might keep going and plummet six floors on to the shoppers below. Could you park and then climb out of the roof? Yes, but how to close the roof afterwards if you don't have one of those very swish cars that does it for you? And then, how would you get back in? Could you climb out of the roof and leave the roof open? No, because the car alarm would go off. Can you climb out of the window? Time was, maybe, but not these days. Could you, if you have a hatchback, drive in forwards and climb out of the tailgate? Believe me, I've done it.

Eventually you accept the inevitable, park as close as you can to the car next door hoping he'll be able to get in the other side, and then open your door as much as you can and do a sort of limbo dance. Your best suit is rubbing up against the muddy car, your ribcage is being crushed against the edge of the door, and the corner of the window has knocked your specs off before you realise that you've left your briefcase in the back seat. Getting back in is harder than getting out. And all this is going to have cost you £32 by the time you get back tonight. Oh joy, oh bliss, oh fuck.

When you return eight hours later, you've lost the ticket, so the £32 you would have had to pay becomes £45. You originally managed to drive forward into the space, but now there's an estate car sticking too far out of the row behind, thus preventing you from reversing out. After wrestling with the steering wheel for ten minutes and executing a 16-point turn, you're at last en route to freedom.

If you are going up a ramp towards the exit, the person in front of you has had to stop on the slope, and is lurching back alarmingly when trying to do a hill start. Reluctantly you give them as brief as possible a blast on the horn to let them know you are there, but being in a confined space, it sounds like the alarm siren going off inside the vault of Fort Knox. Turns out that the bloke having trouble with his hill start is a Millwall supporter, and you scramble for the central locking device as he gets out of the car and lurches towards you, knuckles trailing along the ground as he approaches.

By the way, remember that this is me abbreviating the multi-storey car park section to avoid repeating what I remember of Bill Bryson's stuff.

To tell you the truth, I got so fed up with all the bloody nonsense involved in driving a car that I now ride a motorbike every day, whatever the weather. I know, I know, you're thinking, sad old menopausal fool with the big Harley he couldn't afford when he was young enough to look good on it. Well, you're only five-sixths right. Sad, yes. Old, nearly. Menopausal, probably. Fool, right. Big Harley? No, it's a big Moto-Guzzi. Have you seen the price of a Harley?

However, that's not very interesting. What is more interesting is that, with Ken having done everything possible to dissuade people from taking their cars into London, more and more people are going in on scooters and motorbikes. The trouble is that it's very dangerous and, unlike France where some roads have special lanes marked out for motorcyclists, the UK won't even allow motorcyclists to use bus lanes. Thus we condemn them to weaving in and out between cars driven by lame-brains, who must have spent a lot of time wondering what those shiny sticky-out mirrors on the left and right are for. And in the unlikely event that you do defy death and probability and get to your destination in one piece, there is nowhere to park.

You can ride round and round and round and round and never find a motorcycle bay with an empty space. When you are in a car and can't find a meter or whatever, you do at least have the choice of going into a very expensive car park. On a bike you can't even do that because they think you're going to skip under the barrier and not pay, so they won't let you in.

This means that sometimes you are quite literally stranded on your bike, with absolutely nowhere at all to put it. Just condemned to go round and round and round until you are far too late for the meeting you went in for, so you give up and go home in a bad temper. And if you do find a motorcycle bay that is full of bikes but has a bit of space on one end, and you nudge your bike into the corner, even if the only thing protruding over the white line is the bike-stand, you'll still get a ticket. Yes, that's right: some rat bastard, shit-head, squid-brain of a traffic warden will stick a £40 fine on your petrol-tank. As you might have gathered, this has happened to me recently.

For the sake of getting on, let's fantasise that you're in your car, have found somewhere to park, and you go in search of somewhere to buy your sweeties.

This in itself is no longer easy. Time was when the local parade of shops contained a butcher, a baker, a greengrocer, a hardware shop, a newsagent, a pharmacy, a launderette, a dry-cleaner, a florist, a fishmonger, a fish and chip shop, maybe a greasy spoon, and a corner shop for your groceries. This was an average local high street. Take a look at that same street today.

Starbucks, Prêt à Manger, Coffee Republic, McDonalds, Starbucks, Estate Agent, Costa Coffee Bar, Kentucky Fried Children, Starbucks, Pizza Express, Café Nero, Estillo, Estate Agent, Starbucks, Halifax Building Society, Est Est Est...oh, and another Starbucks. Oh, and a Burger King. You want to buy groceries? Sorry, you have to drive half a mile out of town and go into the aircraft hangar called Sainsbury's. A newspaper? In the local garage. An electric plug? The B&Q 5 miles that way. Need a dry-cleaner? There's one in Tesco on the trading estate.

And how exactly have these international franchises enhanced the environment and architecture of our local high streets? What has been the contribution of these transcontinental conglomerates to the towns and cities in which we live? Apart, I mean, from the polystyrene packaging and picked-over chicken bones we get to trample underfoot.

Well, what they've done is to turn every high street in Britain into a clone of every other high street in Britain. From Aberdeen to Anglesea to Andover, there's no way of knowing if you are in Scotland, Wales or the West Country. Look up to the second floor and you'll see the top half of a fine Victorian building. Look down and you'll see the same red, white and blue plastic livery and patronising logos and slogans that grace every franchise from Bognor to Beijing, from Moscow to Marrakesh via Montgomery and Margate. Same shit, different town.

Stand back and take a good look at it – and weep.

As we've managed to park the car successfully, we might as well do some other shopping. I hate shopping and do as little of it as I possibly can. Jeremy Clarkson told us that he can manage to avoid going shopping for two years before he begins to wonder if maybe he needs some new jeans. That's a bit better than me; usually I can only last a year or so. In recent years I've tended to wait until the hordes have gone back to work or school in January and then go and buy anything left over in the sales.

My least favourite thing is electronics. That's not because I don't like boys' toys as much as the next overgrown kid; it's because I hate the actual process of buying them. This is something that really makes Grumpy Old Men grumpy.

HIGH-TECH HELL

'The biggest lie that the technology manufacturers sell you is "Plug and go". It's plug and "Fuck me, I don't know what's going on here" and it's hours and hours. "What are you doing in there?" from the kitchen. "I've just bought a new piece of kit, darling, and I'm just sorting it out." And it goes on for weeks, you know. "Plug and go", it's a joke.'

MICHAEL GRADE

Someone once told me that 70 per cent of the people who walk into a well-known electronics store with an intention to purchase leave without buying anything. I was reluctant to believe it because this particular chain of stores is very profitable, and I don't think you can stay in business like that. But you try it and see what you think.

To start off with, the store is packed with stuff. There is too much stock, which is all too 'in your face', and there are too many people walking around scratching their heads and crotches looking at it. Then look at the goods on sale. In every

category of item you want to buy – personal hi-fi, ghetto-blaster, DVD, VHS, wide-screen TV – there are at least half a dozen variations by each of Sony, Sanyo, Panasonic, Philips, Toshiba, Thompson, Aiwa, Hitachi, Grundig, Matsui, sometimes by Pace, and that's not to mention Bang & Olufsen.

Now if that's not enough, have a look at the little cards telling you the difference between them. This one by Sony is £30 more expensive than this one by Sony, and you scan the list of features to try to find out what the difference is. They've both got auto-playback melody woofer; both got hi-fibre intake tweaker valves; they both have MP3 sockets and are wi-fi compatible; they both have Bluetooth within 10 metres, and of course they both make toasted sandwiches the George Forman way. Eventually you get to the end of the features and discover that the more expensive one has dewey-capability funk-dunk, which plainly is worth an extra £30 of anyone's money.

All of these gadgets are discreetly arranged behind glass, so you look around for someone to ask for help. There's a range of totally gormless idiots, average age 17, with gelled hair and loads of acne, who look as though they've been out sniffing glue until 3 a.m. Mostly they will look straight past you, or be on the phone to a mate, but if by chance you've still got enough will-power to stop and ask one of them, he'll be wearing a name-badge saying 'Kev', but will point to Damien, who's the only one who specialises in this particular item.

You glance over in the direction young Kev has pointed, and see a very tall, very thin, very bespectacled 20-year-old, with just slightly more charisma than the salted slug who's just been serving you. He's busy patronising a sad couple who want to buy a new stereo system for their daughter, and there is a queue of five people waiting to speak to him. Guess what you do now? If you're sensible, you get out. On the other hand, if the product is something you've been hankering for, or the old one is broken, you might try to persist with the salted slug. You alight on the Sony because, although it's probably not the best, it's the most expensive.

'I'll have one of these.' The slug pats his pockets for a biro and scribbles down a number on the back of his hand next to the tattoo saying 'Sharon' and, leaving a trail of slime in his wake, heads off towards the stockroom. I'll bet you can't guess what happens next. After five minutes he returns and says, 'We don't have that in stock. We can order it for you but it'll take about ten days.' Since you didn't really care about that particular make or model anyway, you point to the next one along and ask if they have that. He writes down a new number next to the tattoo and heads back towards the stockroom. You call after him, 'And if you haven't got that, I'll have the Panasonic.' Five minutes later he's back. 'We don't have those either.'

'I know what,' and this has actually happened to me a couple of times, 'why don't you tell me what you have got, and I'll choose one of them.' 'Well, as a matter of fact the only one we've got at the moment is the Dimsum.' You glance down. It's the only one that looks complete and total crap and is the last one you wanted. Indeed, it sounds as though it was the last one that every other person who has come in the shop has wanted. 'OK,' you hear yourself saying, 'I'll leave it.' Another occasion when, but for rigorous gun-control laws, you'd be reaching for the Kalashnikov.

In the unlikely event that you have enough determination, or are sufficiently desperate to wait for Damien, be ready to be patronised like never before. The worst thing is if maybe you bought one of these mobile phones from this shop nine months ago and it needs a new battery. This makes Damien's day. He's only too happy to tell you that the manufacturers stopped making these six months ago, and he'll do so in a voice that implies that you've asked if he stocks replacement needles for a wind-up gramophone.

If he's in a more than averagely helpful mood, he'll offer to look it up on the computer to see if anyone is still stocking parts for this Neanderthal device. As he does so, you'll see him slyly pointing you out to another nerd behind the counter. 'You'll never guess what that fossil in the grey jacket and trousers is still using...' Eventually he'll come back shaking his head.

Now we Grumpy Old Men come from the generation that still had 'waste not, want not' ringing in our ears from the post-war years. In our day the idea that something might last for more than about 45 minutes was considered a plus. Nowadays not only is this not a virtue, it's a cause of mirth. The fact that this object you are buying because it is 'cool' will be a laughing stock in six months is an actual selling point. 'Ashamed of your mobile?' asks Paul Merton in the ad. Well, I wasn't, but I guess I am now.

Or maybe you want a piece of advice about your computer, which won't print and keeps telling you that it doesn't recognise the printer, rather as our government might decide not to recognise the new government in Azerbaijan. This is going to make his day. 'Is the qwerty cord properly attached to the drexler nozzle?' 'I'm not really sure.' 'Well, you've really got to make sure that the P2T socket has got the nimbo-stratus extension and not the cumulus free-stander. Otherwise you might have overloaded the circuit lozenge and the whole thing will need to be renewed.' You nod, hoping you'll eventually be able to glean some sense out of the occasional word you understood – like 'socket', 'not' and maybe even 'circuit'.

'So I probably need a new printer, then?'

'Yes, probably.'

'Have you got one in stock?'

'No, but you can order one and it should be here in ten days' time.'

Pass the flame-thrower.

TAKE YOUR CHOICE

'I didn't taste pasta till I was a grown man. I didn't taste rice till I was grown up. Most sauces were completely unknown to me. The only product involving tomatoes that came into my life was ketchup. We had brown food and green food and ice cream and that was about it.'

BILL BRYSON

When we were lads, we'd go over to the bakers for a loaf of bread, and there'd be a choice of brown or white. If you were lucky, you might have a choice of sliced or unsliced. Butter? Well, you could have butter or Stork margarine.

Or take something as simple as shampoo. Time was when it was just shampoo. Then it was shampoo for dry, normal or greasy hair. Cool. Then for permed or fly-away hair. Cooler still. Then anti-dandruff. Seems a good idea. Then for hair that's been in the sun too long. OK, I'm still with you. Or especially for blonde hair; now I'm beginning to get just a little bit cynical: how can washing blonde hair be any different from washing brown hair? There's shampoo for hair with split ends – presumably containing glue to stick the ends back together.

Shampoo for hair that's been dyed, and shampoo for hair that's been dyed and is returning to normal. There's shampoo for highlighted hair and for low-lighted hair. Shampoo for fine, thick or frizzy hair. And that's not to mention 'wash and go'. The shampoo shelves in the supermarket used to have about three varieties across 6 inches of shelf space. Now it's 6 feet across and five shelves deep and it takes you half an hour to find the one you want.

We are plagued by the tyranny of choice. Too much thinking to do. Someone recently did an experiment in a supermarket in which they invited customers to sample jam and then take a 'buy one, get one free' (what advertisers refer to aptly as a BOGOF). In the first week they had a table with six varieties on it, in the second they had 24 varieties. It seems that more people were attracted to the table when there were 24 types than when there were 6 types, but only one-tenth as many people went on to actually buy some jam. There was too much choice.

We think more choice makes us happy, but in fact it does the opposite. If we have a choice of two, we know which one we prefer, we choose it and get on. If we have a choice of 12, we don't know which one to choose, so often we won't choose any. And if we do choose, we're tormented by concern that one of the other 11 might have been better.

Meanwhile, supermarkets and manufacturers still believe that the more they put on show, the more we will buy. That's why supermarkets are now the size of aircraft hangars, and it takes two and a half hours to buy enough stuff for a family for three days. Last time I made the mistake of volunteering to go to Tesco (some five years ago, admittedly, at Christmas) I came out reeling. I mean it. Actually dizzy. When I die and go to my own personal hell, that's what it's going to be like. Hyper-illuminated by a quarter of a million striplights, continuous muzak being piped directly into your brain and only interrupted by the soothing tones of the store manager describing this week's 'special purchases'. Thousands of people of all shapes and sizes (so long as it's large), all frantic, all pushing trolleys with squeaky wheels, with scores of frustrated and vile children, selecting brands of soft drinks full of E-numbers, which explains why they are fat, yellow and having temper tantrums because they aren't being allowed to buy a bar of chocolate the size of a semi-detached house.

And what about sell-by dates? That's a good one, isn't it? When they were first introduced we all thought, 'That'll keep the manufacturers and the shopkeepers on their toes – now they'll have to ensure that everything is fresh'. How stupid could we be? Because what it's actually become is the retail equivalent of the telephone answering machine. Time was when you'd phone a mate, he wasn't in, so you put down the phone and save the cost of the phone call. Now he isn't in, but the phone is answered anyway, so you get to pay the phone company even though you don't actually get to speak to the person you wanted to speak to. And the same thing happens when you phone him later. And later again. But sell-by dates: how much food that is perfectly OK, absolutely fine, gets thrown out every day because it's a day past its sell-by date? This drives me demented. People squinting at little labels on perfectly good food and throwing it out because it's a day or two past its sell-by date.

There's now a sandwich shop that claims it throws away sandwiches if they've been on the shelves for three hours. I want to ask the guy behind the counter for a sandwich that's three hours and five minutes old so that I won't have to pay for it. Thus far I haven't, but I sense that the day is not far off...

I should probably admit that I might tend to go just a little bit the other way here. Recently my wife had to physically stop me from giving someone a can of beer I found in the back of the cupboard that was two years past its sell-by date. But what the hell? It's beer. It's in a can. If there's anything wrong with it, the drinker will work it out at the first sip. No, sell-by dates have turned into a bonanza for food manufacturers – because we're all mugs.

Anyway, back in the supermarket, eventually you get to the checkout. Now I'm the first to admit that women are better than men at just about everything I can think of, but why is it that when they get to the front of the queue at the checkout, they don't realise that they have to pay? How many times have you seen it? She's been queuing for half an hour and watching people pack their stuff into bags, pay their bills and move on. She has then stood and packed 100 items into 15 plastic carrier bags. Then, when the cashier says, 'That'll be £72.20,' she looks amazed. 'Oh, yes,' she says, and starts patting her pockets and looking in the bowels of her handbag for her cheque-book. Then she needs a pen. Then she writes out the cheque, stopping to ask the date. Then the checkout assistant stamps the cheque with the name of the supermarket. Then the cheque guarantee card has to be unearthed.

Yep, grocery shopping is not for me.

SHEDLOADS OF DIY

'I really get fascinated in supermarkets – there is this particular type of woman – they have to get the food divider – if you're in front of them, taking out your groceries, they have to get the food divider really, really quickly so they can start unpacking their bag…sometimes what I do is actually angle

*my body so they can't get it. You know, it's like,
"Why are you so desperate to get this food divider
thing?"*

FELIX DEXTER

So before we get on with our day, let's pause for a little moment
to consider DIY hypermarkets. IKEA came in for a bit of a
beating in the first *Grumpy Old Men* TV series, and naturally this
Scandinavian version of hell is totally out of bounds for
grumpies in any but the most extreme of circumstances. But
what is going on in DIYFS – or Do It Your Fucking Self, as I
habitually call it – do you suppose?

I have now made it a life rule that in no circumstances will
I go to one of these places on a Saturday – not even if I have
finally managed to run out of excuses not to put this mirror on
the wall, and am desperate for a new drill-bit or some
Rawlplugs. I wouldn't go in there on a Saturday for my
barbecue briquettes if Dame Edna Everidge herself was coming
round for a barbie.

Now one thing I've never done in my life is to manage a
retail store. I've certainly worked in them as a student, but I've
never had to produce the staff roster. However, even without
having completed the Retail Studies Degree Course at the
Kenny Everett School of Break-Dancing, I think I'd be able to
work out that Saturday was going to be a big day for DIY. I
think I'd therefore try to organise the roster so that one or two
of my staff turned up on a Saturday.

This seems to be beyond the capabilities of the people who
run the local hardware supermarkets. Sometimes there are a few
members of staff around on a Saturday in DIYFS; it's just that
none of them is serving. There are uniformed people filling up
shelves, on the phone, running around looking harassed, and
standing in groups discussing whether Kylie, who's just started

in plumbing, might be up for a quickie in the stockroom. The trouble is that none of them are on the bloody tills.

So you get a queue of literally dozens of people, ranging from proper workmen who have just popped in for a bit of extra lagging to finish the plumbing job at number 32, to couples who've come in to buy some bedding plants, to downtrodden husbands who have enough tubes and pipes and radiators on their trolleys to replumb the outside of the London Stock Exchange. Meanwhile, at the front of the queue someone who wants a packet of runner-bean seeds has chosen one without a bar-code, and the harassed-looking Asian woman at the checkout has rung her bell and is holding up the packet waiting for one of her colleagues to come to the rescue.

Eventually they do, they grab the packet of seeds and head off into the deepest, darkest depths of the warehouse towards the aisle displaying the runner-bean seeds to try to find a packet with a bar-code that works. Everything stops. Everyone waits. Someone at the back of the queue is beginning to get a bit tetchy. They get into a deliberately loud conversation with the people in front of them. Why aren't any of the 14 other people managing the tills? Finally, one person in the queue ostentatiously gives up, drops their stuff on the counter and walks out. All these stores have installed those automatic doors because they were so sick of people slamming them on the way out.

At last a new packet of runner-bean seeds with a proper bar-code will be produced, and a satisfied customer, who could have grown the seeds into a beanstalk and run off and married the bloody giant in the time she's taken to buy them, leaves the store. The next customer has bought some plastic tubing, which has also lost its magnetic strip, and you see the beleaguered assistant reaching for a large loose-leaf binder featuring a range of instruments of destruction. With more hope than optimism, you watch them try to match up the item they have in their hand with the line-drawing of it in the manual. Yes, they've got everything but… The manager is called. Someone rushes off back to the shelves to try to find a similar piece of pipe, and the whole merry-go-round starts again.

So who is in charge of this bloody shambles? Well, it happens that an old mate of mine called Roy is now quite *un grand fromage* in DIYFS. When he first got the job my wife put in jeopardy our very good friendship by asking Roy what she thought was the simple question, 'Why don't the shop assistants in your stores water the plants?' Roy is a very kind and patient man, but I thought the twitch in his face more eloquent than anything he could have said. In the event, he confined himself to, 'We're trying to fix that,' and we went on to other things.

MOBILE TYRANNY

'I'd love to have one of those phones that takes photographs to be able to send them to your children, you know, "This is Daddy" or whatever. But I've got two problems. One is that I'm always listening to dance remixes. The second is that as soon as somebody starts to instruct me, I start to get prickly. And I don't know what it is, but I've always been like that. Hate being taught.'

JOHN PEEL

So anyway, you're trying to have a couple of minutes to yourself before resuming your journey when you hear that familiar anthem that has so far provided the soundtrack to the 21st century. Diddle dee dah, diddle dee dah, diddle dee dah dah. That's the best I can render it in words, but you know exactly what I mean. The most popular of the seemingly thousands of different ways of irritating us that have been dreamed up by mobile phone operators and allied youth. Nowadays it's everything from whistling birds to a whinnying horse, from Justin Timberlake to a steamship whistle. Heaven knows, I even heard one the other day that sounds like an old-fashioned telephone ringing. I suppose that's called 'retro'.

Does anyone else remember when it was possible to 'just disappear' for a few hours? I used regularly to take the train journey from London to Manchester, and although for a whole range of reasons it was often a living hell, you did at least hear people saying, 'It's the only chance I get to read a book' or even 'It's the one chance I get to think'. Or, sometime around about 1970, it seems to me that you could go for a drive in the country and if domestic or work-related mayhem had broken out, you at least would be spared the knowledge of it until you got home.

In those days, if you saw someone walking down the street or sitting alone in a car talking out loud, they were probably a case for what we these days call 'care in the community'. Talking to oneself used to be a definition of lunacy.

The first mobile phone I came across was so big and heavy that it had to be carried on a strap over someone's shoulder, and a wire connected the handset to a very large black box. It weighed the same as a Sherman tank and the batteries lasted about half an hour. Then, when they started coming down in size a bit, there was that phase where just a few people had them, and my, my, what a bloody fuss they did make. Do you remember? Characters who all looked like estate agents, and probably were, ostentatiously standing in the street shouting into something that looked like a walkie-talkie. We were all supposed to be impressed, but even then we all thought they looked like wankers.

Then it started happening on trains. You'd be just dozing off to the soporific rhythm of the wheels on the track when you'd hear someone shouting, 'Hello? Hello? Yes, it's me. Mark. Yes, I'm on the train. Yes, one of those new mobile phone things. Yes, they're marvellous, aren't they? Hello? Hello? Hello? Oh yes, you're still there. Has John managed to take a look at the tender documents for the secret project yet?' In fact, the line would have been broken half a mile ago, but the man on the train would pretend to continue talking rather than have other travellers know that the gadget he is making such an exhibition of is in fact a piece of crap.

Those were the days, weren't they? You had to make about 20 attempts just to complete a single phone call. And how many times did you find yourself talking for five minutes before you realised that you'd been cut off? When you eventually realised you'd call back and say, 'Where did you lose me?' and it would turn out that it was five minutes earlier and he's been trying to call you back but you've been engaged, speaking into the empty cosmos.

I never actually did it, but on several occasions I came about one and a half seconds away from throwing my mobile phone out of the window of a moving car. Such was the frustration of continually dialling up, getting through, establishing where you'd got to when you'd been cut off, then resuming, only to be cut off again. Eventually you just react by wanting to get the bloody thing as far away from you as you could. But just before you do it, just before it stonks off the central reservation and explodes into a thousand pieces, you do a quick mental balance sheet of the momentary satisfaction involved in doing so against the much longer-term irritation of dealing with the consequences.

It's a bit like losing your temper and throwing a plate through the window – exquisitely delicious for about three seconds, but what a pain in the neck to have to deal with.

I bet mine's smaller than yours! ...

And it occurs to me just now that this is an example of what we were talking about earlier – all that AGA rubbish. When you're younger maybe you'll give in to the impulse, lose your temper, do something stupid and then spend days picking up the pieces. When you are old you just sigh and get on with it. But in that middle period – in your grumpy years – you've experienced enough of those 'act in haste, repent at leisure' moments, and would prefer to exercise restraint rather than let it all out in a single flashpoint. With age comes wisdom. The trouble is that instead of letting it all out in a flash of temper, you bottle it up and wind up muttering and mumbling to yourself. What you've actually managed to do is to store up another huge weight of grump to be downloaded gradually on to the poor sods unfortunate enough to have chosen to share their lives with you.

Nowadays we are practically fetishistic about our mobile phones. Rick Stein reflected how amusing it is that men are apparently constantly worried about having the largest willy, but are preoccupied with having the smallest phone. Rick may inadvertently have given us more of an insight into what makes him tick than he intended, but let's leave that to one side. Bill Nighy went on to admit that he doesn't care what make of phone he has, so long as it's the smallest. My mobile is about three years old and is the size and weight of half a brick, and don't think I haven't noticed the barely disguised smirks of anyone under the age of 30 when they see it. Do I care? Well, I suppose I do a bit; it's just that I don't care quite enough to go through all the utterly exhausting crapulence of having to exchange it.

It's not so much the walking into the shop and asking about a new mobile that I object to, it's having to fend off all the claptrap about comparative features and packages. And then it's having to say no to all the bolt-ons that these patronising salesmen – it seems always to be men – have been incentivised to put you through.

'Would you like to choose one of our range of outer cases designed to make your phone look like anything from a bar of Cadbury's Dairy Milk to a *Star Trek* phaser?'

'No, thank you.'

'Would you like the extended warranty that guarantees replacement if the device is lost or stolen within 36 months?'

'No, thank you.'

'Would you like the handy carrying case in luxury hand-tooled skivertex?'

'No, thank you. I just want the bloody phone. Now will you take my credit card, let me sign it and allow me to get the hell out of here?'

'Yes, of course, sir, but I just have to ask you…'

Too late, I'm gone. Destined to live with my half-brick for another six months, or at least until I can summon up the forbearance to pay another visit to the phone shop. But I know that I have to go back sometime. And they'll be waiting.

Do you hate it when you go into a shop to buy something and they ask you your address? I just want to buy a new radio, and the bloke behind the counter wants to know where I live. 'What's that got to do with you?' I've asked many times. 'It's for the guarantee,' they say. 'I don't need to give you my address for a guarantee,' I say, 'I just need proof of purchase.' The poor sod behind the counter looks skywards, and occasionally I've felt so sorry for him – just trying to do his job for some total bastard of a store manager – that I've acquiesced and given my address.

'What's the house number?' Now for years I didn't know our house had a number. We live in one of those poncey culs-de-sac with about four houses in it, which all have a name and no number. Eventually I found that this caused such distress that I asked the postman, and he said it was number 2.

'Two', I reply.

'Postcode?'

I give them the postcode, and within one and a half seconds they have my full address. When that first happened to me I thought that was very weird. Yet another 'big brother' moment. I suppose I might have expected the Special Branch to be able to access my full address, but the fact that they can do it in Comet was a bit of a surprise.

'Phone number?' I always draw the line there, and I guess a lot of other people must do the same because they never remonstrate. Can you imagine just tucking into your fish fingers, the phone rings and it's someone from Comet asking you if you'd like to update that hi-fi you bought three months ago and is now so embarrassingly out of date?

I asked Bob Geldof if he ever receives phone calls at home from someone trying to sell him double glazing. 'I do,' he said without fear or favour, 'and I tell them to fuck off.'

Anyway, the mobile is ringing and it's my good wife (needless to say, before you ask, I don't also have a bad wife). It seems that the McKinseys are coming over to dinner, and would I drop by the deli and pick up some 'foccacio' – whatever that is. I used to like it when your friends would pop round more or less unannounced and you'd knock up a quick spaghetti bolognese or maybe push the boat out and get a Chinese take-away and get trounced by a couple of bottles of cheap white wine.

Nowadays the people we mix with don't do that. Every social occasion is a major undertaking. On the rare occasions that we have people around to dinner at our place, the house goes on to a war footing five to seven days in advance.

The entire place has to be cleaned from top to bottom – even though our guests have no reason to go upstairs and never do. Meat starts to marinate three days ahead, and there is usually a 'Plan B' just in case we lose heart with the 'Plan A' recipe. All the cutlery and plates we own have a special wash, tablecloths come out of drawers to be pressed, the best napkins are laundered and ironed. She even changes the beds – what sort of party she's thinking it might turn into defeats me.

Delia is all over every work surface, with maybe Jamie doing the starters and Nigella doing the dessert. Or possibly the other way round. Sometimes, indeed, a main-course recipe can be a hybrid between Jamie and Nigella – what on earth would the tabloids say?

Lots of different sizes and shapes of bread roll appear in the bread bin, and half a dozen varieties of cheese appear in the fridge – and don't even think about cutting yourself a piece. There are cheeses from many English counties and many European nations, some with chives, some with mould, some with blue streaks through it, some with pinkish streaks, some with a crust and some liquid at room temperature.

As the hour approaches, the tension mounts; crudités appear alongside three different varieties of dip, olives and hand-cooked crisps are dispensed into bowls, all the glasses get a wash and polish, and so it goes on and on. Fallen leaves are swept from the drive, carpets get a last-minute run-around with the vacuum cleaner, candles are lit, music is selected and I find that my most expensive wine has been put in the fridge. I swear to God, there was less fuss made in the preparations for the coronation of the King of Tonga. My wife even keeps a little book to ensure that she doesn't give the same guests the same food twice.

'Like they'd remember,' I say, rather stupidly.

'Nicola would,' says my wife.

'I'll bet that Peter wouldn't,' I say.

'Yeah, well, that's men for you.' I should have known better.

And all this for our close friends: imagine what would happen if someone who mattered was coming?

I realised the other day that this is one of the sure signs of grumpiness. When the relief you feel after your friends have gone is so enjoyable that it outweighs the pain in the arse of having them visit in the first place. A shocking thing to say? I know, but hey, if I'm bothering to write this down, I might as well be honest.

Time was when some friends or relatives coming around would be a high spot on your social calendar. You might even look forward to it. However, what I started to realise was that, after the ordeal was over and our guests had waved goodbye and shouted 'Lovely evening, must do it again soon' out of the window of their departing car, I would sit down on the settee with the dregs of a bottle of wine and enjoy a few minutes of unvarnished pleasure. A rare thing in the life of a grumpy.

'Well, thank Christ that's over.'

My wife is horrified. 'What are you talking about? That was a lovely evening – and they're your friends.'

So now my brief moment of pleasure is over because already I'm feeling guilty. It's true that they are my friends more than hers. It's true that she's gone to enormous, and I mean enormous, trouble to make the evening go well. So why have I not enjoyed myself? Because all the while my pleasure at having them visit is overlaid by the running commentary that's going on in my head.

'What does it matter if it was Thursday or Friday? I wish he'd get to the bloody point.' 'Does she realise that I don't know "Irene from accounts" or "Johnson from marketing", so the fact that they're having an affair couldn't possibly be a subject of greater indifference to me?' 'Is he really going to list every single one of the engine parts he had to dismantle in order to get to the rocker-gasket in the overhead camshaft? Yes, he is.' 'I wonder if he is ever going to get to the end of this story about his sodding stupid oldest son who has just been selected to be among the three people out of 17 million applicants for a scholarship at Stowe.' 'I think she's ageing a lot better than he is: I wonder if he's ageing better than me.'

Yes, it's appalling. These are my friends. People I actually like. What would happen if we entertained someone I objected to? And admit it, you do it too, I bet. And if you don't, it just makes me a worse person than I thought I was, and everyone else better than I think they are.

WORK BECKONS

Back to the car and a quick glance at the headlines before we set off. Robin Cook blasts the government over the decision to invade Iraq. Whoah! That'll rock them to their foundations – a blast from Robin Cook. Can anyone explain Robin Cook to me? How could we possibly have got to the point in the first decade of the 21st century when anyone on the planet is in the remotest bit interested in what Robin Cook has to say about anything?

Last time I looked Robin Cook was the foreign secretary.

You'd switch on the news and see him waddling down the steps of an aircraft to be met by 'his opposite number' in some foreign state. Wouldn't it be funny if 'his opposite number' was also a gnome, and you had a newsreel shot of two gnomes hugging on the tarmac, then falling over backwards and giggling. Unfortunately, the poor hapless sod sent to greet Robin Cook was usually not a gnome, and was probably a reasonably sensible person, trying to do a reasonable job, whose week was disrupted by an unsolicited visit from a character from Tolkien who's coming to see you just so he can get his picture in the papers back home.

Look at some of these blokes, then ask yourself why it is that the turn-out at elections is at the lowest point since the war. When I were a lad (imagine this being said against the background of the Hovis music) I used to go to the Durham Miners' Gala to have a picnic on the one sunny day in the whole northeast summer. We would sit on the grass and listen to Tony Benn haranguing the assembled multitudes. He would talk about old-fashioned stuff you never hear any more – things like international brotherhood and workers' rights. Seems kind of quaint, don't you think? He'd talk about justice, right and wrong, fairness, that sort of thing (are you still mentally dubbing in the Hovis music?). Or you might see Michael Foot, ranting away like some Old Testament prophet, but with a sense of commitment and integrity that touched a chord somewhere deep inside you.

We remembered John F. Kennedy telling Americans, 'Ask not what your country can do for you, ask rather what you can do for your country.' And Martin Luther King dreaming dreams that sounded as though they had been inscribed by forked lightning on tablets of marble and were being brought down from the mountain. We had posters of Che Guevara on our walls, marched to ban the bomb, and rioted in Grosvenor Square.

Kids the same age as I was then now turn on the telly and see Oliver Letwyn. If you know who Oliver Letwyn is, I need say no more. If not, just imagine someone so wet he looks as though he might transubstantiate at any moment. Or Ian McCartney – no doubt an able and sincere bloke, but who on earth is going to follow him into the trenches? With the best will in the world, we can't even understand what he says, let alone believe in it.

Or John Redwood? You must remember him. John Redwood on that conference platform in Wales – when he was secretary of state for Wales – and the whole company is singing the Welsh national anthem, except that he doesn't know the words, so he's mouthing them and looking terrified. Whenever I see something like that I wonder what he must have done to piss off his civil servants so much that they let him get himself into that situation. Nothing will persuade me that someone in his department didn't see that coming. They always sing the Welsh national anthem at the end of such gatherings, and some very senior person in John Redwood's office will have known it, foreseen what was going to happen and decided not to tell him, thereby making him a look a complete and utter divi. 'That'll teach him to make me give up my holidays to write his speech,' someone is thinking. Or maybe they're not, but it amuses me to imagine it.

By now you might be just about as relieved as I am that I've finally arrived at work. First things first, pick up the messages on the answering machine and turn on the computers. Yep, listen to the Worldwide Windows anthem – a daily global homage to Bill Gates – same jingle, playing in tens of millions of offices and homes all around the planet.

Get into the email. Yes, good, I've typed the wrong password. Put in the correct one. That's it. Oops, I've put a comma instead of a full stop between my name. Try again. Oh dear, I've typed .con instead of .com. Get it right this time. Yes, yes, here we go – 27 new messages. Let's have a look.

Seems I've won $25,000 and all I have to do is to enter a prize draw to collect it. Thanks. Delete. An invitation from someone I've never heard of in Las Vegas to have sex with his sister. Kind of you to offer, but delete. Personalised logos for small businesses by return. Good, thank you, delete. College girls do it for the first time. I daresay, but I think that's rather a matter for them, don't you? Delete. Save 25 per cent off my car insurance. Not just now, thanks. Delete. Teenage girls go down on the farm. I'm sure they do. Nice offer but I couldn't possibly accept. Delete. Four or five from names I recognise, but including an enclosure that looks as though it might be a virus. Thanks, delete. Ebony hoes – they say black girls don't suck. Do they, indeed? I didn't know they said that. Never too late to learn something new. Thanks anyway. Delete. Oh, here's one from my accountant. The VAT returns are due. Excellent. Delete.

Now I'm as fond of a bit of harmless pornography as the next sad old bastard, but you can eventually get paranoid about receiving all these ever more vile email messages. I mean, when I first used to get them I found some of them vaguely titillating, but honestly, most of them nowadays are truly, truly horrible. I mean seriously horrible. And it seems that I inadvertently compounded my inbox problem by once or twice clicking on the 'please remove me' button, which I'm now told may remove you from that particular database, but ensures that your address is sold on to 100 more. So now if anyone looks over my shoulder when I'm opening my mail, they immediately have me down as a pervert. Wonderful.

What in the world did we do before email? If the email goes down in our office, it's as though there's been a death in the family. Or maybe the building has been covered in rubble and we're cut off from the world. Everyone sits around and mopes until it comes back on again, and then they all come back to life.

Now and again, to while away the dark hours while the email is down, I treat everybody to one of my fascinating stories of the olden days – like the one about the origin of the expression 'cut and paste'. You may wonder what I mean – what could possibly be unclear about 'cut and paste'? But that's because you probably come from a generation that played with paper, paste and scissors in primary school – whereas most of the current generation came across the expression as a word-processing term long after it was ever a physical activity, if it ever was.

If you don't get this, it's probably because you are so out of touch that you think Big Brother is a character from Orwell and that a virus is a way of catching a disease.

Anyhow, cut and paste. They all sit around, their eyes wide with wonder, as I tell them about the time when I started work as a producer on the *World in Action* series. In those days we'd come back from a location with dozens of reels of ¼-inch magnetic tape, and all the transcripts of the interviews had to be typed on manual typewriters. Indeed, four copies would be made, using something we used to call carbon paper. Two young women, Marian and Barbara, would sit in front of huge machines, their fingers a blur, bashing out scores of pages of dialogue. You never heard about repetitive strain injury in those days. (Marian went on to be my PA for 13 years – hello, Marian.)

Producers would draw a circle round the paragraphs of the interview they wanted to use, and type bits of commentary on blank sheets of paper. They would leave gaps, about the size of the paragraph of dialogue they wanted to insert. Then they would get a pair of scissors, cut out the paragraphs they wanted from the interviews and Sellotape or staple them in between the paragraphs of commentary. Cut and paste. You'd be left with a huge tangle of paper, which you would have to photocopy to get a decent working document.

We put our programmes together in Manchester, but our lawyers were in London, and since our programme was broadcast on a Monday night, we pretty much had to get a script to them the preceding Friday. So we would refine and change and cross out and endlessly photocopy and re-photocopy the script until the last possible moment, and then send it by post or, *in extremis*, by train on Thursday night. With luck it would arrive on Friday morning, be read by our legal advisers, and all the rest of the discussions would take place on the phone with the lawyer trying to decipher a barely legible page with practically invisible bits of script and dialogue typed on it. The lawyers had no chance to see the actual pictures that went with the words because they were on film, but that's another story.

All that versus what we do today – cut, paste, save, close, attach and send – 20 seconds. There, I think you can see why everyone in our office finds these stories mesmerising.

'Anyone want a cappuccino?' one of them will ask, almost as though they need something to bring them round. Since the email still isn't back on, it's unilaterally decided that everyone will go out to Starbucks.

TEA OR COFFEE?

'Starbucks makes pretty good coffee. That's got to be a good thing. But it's all those newspapers and "Hey, wow" sofas, and the pain au raisin that goes with it that I can't stand. So the fact that you can get a decent cup of coffee in any high street – a good thing. All the bollocks that goes with it – fuck off.'

BOB GELDOF

Nowadays Starbucks is the most ubiquitous representative of US cultural imperialism, having largely taken over the role from McDonalds. There now seem to be almost as many Starbucks as estate agents, and I don't think I can put my opinion of it any better than did Bob Geldof.

Unfortunately, I can't endorse his premise that they make pretty good coffee because I don't drink coffee, and they've gone to as much trouble as possible to make you feel a prat being the only person in the queue asking for tea. It's like you've gone into a Boots in Harrogate and asked for ribbed condoms. I always say it as softly as I think I can get away with, and they repeat it loudly. 'Tea? What size?'

'Small.'

Of course, they don't do anything called small. The smallest they do is what I would call large. Their medium is an ice-bucket, their large would put out the Great Fire of London. But here's the thing that I want to know. When did it become OK, when you asked for a cup of tea, to put a teabag into a paper cup, pour hot water on it and hand it to you? When did that become OK?

Now let's go back a little bit here because this goes to the

essence of grump. Tea. It's our national drink. Do you remember? Just like 'cut and paste', it's not that long ago. And like 'cut and paste', it may all seem obvious to you, but is worth recording just in case there is a nuclear holocaust and this is the only book left in the world describing the decline and fall of the human race.

'Would you like a cup of tea, sir?'

'Yes, thank you.'

'Won't be a moment'.

Someone goes to a tap and fills up a kettle. Oh, that's good, it means the water is going to be freshly boiled. You wait five minutes, during which time a teapot, preferably made of china, is warmed with a little hot water. Then leaves of loose tea are spooned into it, one spoonful per person, and 'one for the pot'. The bubbling water is poured directly on to the tea leaves.

You receive the teapot and china, wait another five minutes, maybe stirring the brew once, then pour the tea through a strainer into the cup. You can then spend a happy five minutes discussing the merits of pouring the milk in the cup before or after the tea. Then it's time for your second cup.

And kids today don't believe you when you tell them how hard we worked.

Today in Starbucks you queue for 20 minutes behind a long line of cycle messengers or women with babies in slings around their necks, ordering a skinny latte or a cappuccino or a large expresso or a macchiato. (That's the messengers and women, not the babies.) Eventually someone from Prague asks you what you want: you ask for tea and it's not quite clear if they have heard you or not. The person you have spoken to disappears in the mêlée, and while they are away, three other people from various parts of eastern Europe ask you what you want. You tell them you are being served. After about ten minutes you notice that the person you thought was serving you is serving someone else, so you try to catch her eye. She gestures towards the far end of the counter, and it turns out that your 'tea' has been standing in front of the till for the last five minutes.

You pick up a half-gallon container made of cardboard, scald your hands and go to the chest-height circle of Formica that substitutes for a table. You take off the plastic top and the hot liquid spills over the side of the cup. There are no napkins to wipe it up. The teabag is still in the water, but no milk. You look around. Eventually you spot a scrum of messengers and mothers in the far corner, and just where the rugby ball would be is where you are supposed to serve yourself with milk and sugar. You walk across and someone takes your place at the Formica circle, and your only consolation is to see them put their sleeve into your spilt tea. The string attached to the teabag has fallen into the cup, and you look for something to fish it out. There is a long wooden stick, but nowhere to put the hot and soggy teabag. You select from stainless steel flasks full of semi-skimmed or full-fat milk. The one you want is empty, so you use the other one. Now there is nowhere to sit, so you stand to one side, trying not to get in the way of the pushchairs. You take a mouthful.

Well, it may be hot, it may be wet, it may sometimes even be reasonably refreshing. What is sure as hell is not is tea.

NANNY KNOWS BEST

'I've had hypnotherapy, acupuncture, people hitting me with twigs, I had another man who electrocuted me every time I had a fag. That didn't stop me. Oh dear, it's a terrible thing. Grumpy Old Man? This is my sixth day without a cigarette and I could rip your fucking head off.'

ARTHUR SMITH

No, I don't go out to Starbucks when the email is down. What I do is take a walk during lunchtime so that the younger people in the office can discuss what a senile old git I am without having to whisper. To get out of the building you have to step over a small mound of cigarette butts that is now a permanent feature in the doorway of any public building.

When I see that it always takes me back 40 years to the guys behind the bike sheds cultivating their James Dean image by taking a furtive drag on anything from a straw to a Woodbine, which the corner shop used to sell in ones. The shop was owned by a man who constantly dribbled, so there was a danger that the fags were a bit soggy, but that's probably too much information.

These guys dreamed of growing up so they could smoke

where and when they liked, and look cool and sophisticated, just like the film stars did. This was in the days when your mental image of smokers was more Marlon Brando than someone coughing their lungs out. But that of course pre-dated the 'we know much better than you do what's good for you' bollocks we all have to put up with these days.

Certainly it was right that the minute anyone understood that smoking was bad for us that we should be told about it. Certainly it was a good thing to put up the scary posters in schools and hospitals, and though I regard it as generally intrusive to put a dying person in your living room without notice, it's even appropriate to put anti-smoking advertisements on the telly. I also think it's a little heavy-handed to make people carry around a cigarette packet that's labelled 'Smoking kills'. However, if that's necessary to make sure that people understand the risks they are taking, then that's also fine with me. Whatever we can do to make sure that children and adults are aware of the reality of what smoking does to them we should do.

But when we've told people about the problem, and we have, there must come a point when grown-ups should be allowed to make up their own minds. They're grown up. It's their funeral, quite literally, so where does the government get off hounding people with a nicotine habit so that they are now made to feel like criminals?

Nowadays you can't smoke in many public places, and so you see dozens of harassed and hunted-looking people, summer and winter, rain or shine, standing outside offices up and down the land, inhaling as much nicotine as they can in a short time as if their lives depended on it, which, of course, in an oddly reversed sort of way, it does.

These were the same guys who used to ride their motorbikes or scooters down to Brighton on a bank holiday for the annual punch-up between mods and rockers – without wearing a crash-helmet. Because in those days if you wanted to cave your skull in when you fell off your machine, this was thought to be unwise, but was left largely as a matter for oneself to decide. It's my skull, if I want to crack it open, isn't that rather a matter for me?

And these must be the same guys who used to have the freedom to crash through their windscreens if they bumped their car into a tree at anything more than about 15 miles per hour. Obviously there were plenty of warnings about the dangers of not wearing seat-belts, but in those days you were allowed to decide for yourself if you liked that attractive Frankenstein-style sewn-together look. Nowadays someone else has decided that for us.

Of course, that was only if you were a front-seat passenger, but then some busybody decided that too many rear-seat passengers were becoming front-seat passengers a little too speedily in the event of a head-on collision, and introduced a law requiring rear-seat passengers to wear a seat-belt as well. Because obviously that's too complicated a decision for us to be allowed to make for ourselves.

Short of grabbing the same oversized builder's trowel we used on page 14 and laying this on any thicker, it may be that you are beginning to get my drift. The days when we were regarded as more or less independent-minded grown-ups, to be educated and properly informed about the dangers of the environment around us, but then left to make our own decisions, are gone.

You might be tempted to say that it's the State's business because the State has to deal with the mess your mangled body makes on the pavement. But that's to ignore the simple economic truth that dying young does the State a favour. It's those of us who live to a ripe old age who become a huge burden on it. A fast death wrapped round a lamppost may be messy, but at least it's cheap.

No, these days the health and safety fascists have taken over. In our business we have to produce a 40-page 'risk assessment' if we want to clean the windows. School trips are being cancelled because the teachers don't necessarily want their faces plastered all over the front pages of the tabloids if there should be an accident and one of their charges is hurt. You can't get insurance for the village bonfire party, so hundreds of years of tradition have – well, I was going to say 'gone up in smoke', but of course that's exactly what it hasn't done. It's been extinguished.

This is all familiar territory – but the aspect of the nanny state that just creases me up every time it happens – I just can't get used to it – is in the pharmacy. Go into a busy high street chemist and ask to buy some paracetamol, then watch what happens. The person behind the counter will hold up the box and shout 'Paracetamol' at the top of their lungs. The overworked pointy-head behind the serving hatch at the back will glance up, look you up and down for a split second and nod their head. Despite yourself, you feel a momentary beam of satisfaction that you have been deemed suitable to be allowed to purchase some paracetamol.

Now what, for the love of God, is the pharmacist looking for in that split second? How exactly do you qualify as someone who won't be allowed to buy paracetamol? What does a paracetamol addict look like? What does a potential suicide-by-paracetamol look like?

They can't even seriously be looking to see if you've been in recently to buy paracetamol: first, this happens in the busiest chemists in the land, where they couldn't possibly be expected to remember you. Second, if you were a serious paracetamol hoarder, you would presumably go from one chemist to the next like a strung-out junkie, buying whatever is the upper limit in every store.

And it's not just paracetamol. It's bloody flu remedy and anti-histamine and even aspirin. 'How many?' the assistant asks. 'Fifty?' Then at the top of her lungs she shouts, 'Fifty aspirin!' and you feel as though you've just asked for crack cocaine at the WI or tea in Starbucks. Everyone looks at you to see what sort of creature is so depraved.

When did it become OK for the State to make all these decisions for us? Sure, we're used to the idea that we're not allowed to drink too much when we're driving – that's fair enough because it potentially harms others. We're also used to the idea that the State has an opinion on whether we can smoke dope. But just stand back from it for a minute. What on earth has it got to do with the State if we smoke dope or not?

When this subject gets its regular airing on telly or radio, you hear people asking how it is that since alcohol is more damaging for you than dope, why are you allowed to drink and not allowed to smoke weed? 'Well, if alcohol were introduced now,' the answer comes back, 'it would also be banned.' Well, excuse me, but first, I seem to think that's been tried in one or two earlier times and one or two places, and it has never worked, and second, who exactly are these pontificators?

Maybe it's the same bastards who sit in little council chambers and decide to stop cars cutting through Richmond Park because too many people on their way to a long, hard day in the office were enjoying a brief view of the deer, whose upkeep is coming out of their taxes. We're paying for the park, we're just not allowed to go in it. A bit like Buckingham Palace or Clarence House. The same people who decided one day to stop you turning right where you've been turning right for the last 20 years. The people we couldn't be bothered to stand for election against, or vote against, so we're now being punished for our apathy. Oops, there I go again, forgetting that this is supposed to be lighthearted grumpiness, and instead of that it's turning into the bloody *Anarchists' Gazette*. Better lighten up – or 'chill' as my daughter would say.

My point is, it may be the legitimate role of the State to ensure that all of us know what is good for us and what is bad for us, but then they should back off and allow us to make up our own minds.

It's not that hard to do. Let's see if we can have a go. At double speed.

A little alcohol is good for us, too much is bad for us, so try to stop drinking before you see double. If you drink too much and then drive a car, we're going to put you in prison. OK? Dope is less harmful than alcohol, and doesn't necessarily 'lead on to harder things', but the jury's out and it's maybe better not to do too much. Mountaineering? Fairly dangerous. Lots of people killed and injured, and, worse still, loads of people killed and injured coming to rescue you. If you must do it, make sure you're properly trained and have the right kit. But if you get into trouble, you're on your own. Next? Smoking is definitely harmful, and it would be better not to do it. If you do do it, try to do it away from other people so that you don't endanger them. Cocaine, crack, heroin, etc? Really bad news. Better not to go there. Riding a motorcycle without a crash-helmet? Really silly idea – apart from anything else, your hair looks a mess when you get off – but at least you're not putting anyone else at risk. Skiing? Hundreds of people killed every year and thousands more injured. Better not to do it really, but, again, you need some training if you're going to. And if you don't know what you're doing and you smash into and kill someone else who is minding their own business on the slopes, we're going to put you in prison. Driving without a seat-belt: fairly silly really. The airbags will help, but you're probably better off with both. Caving? Daft idea: loads of people get stuck down holes with the water rising, or break limbs miles under ground, and the poor bastards who have to come to your rescue get hurt too. Go by all means, but if you get stuck, start praying because God is the only one who is going to save you. E? Can cause problems, so always take it with a friend and drink plenty of water. Scuba-diving? Dangerous stuff; loads of people get into difficulties. Water-skiing…? Sky-diving…?

You get the idea. Why not make sure we know what the problem is and then leave us the hell alone?

LOOK AND LEARN

'Here's one – I bought a sofa the other day and I was sent an instruction leaflet on how to use it, which, I presume – I didn't actually open it – but I assume it said you just sit on it. It's what it must have said. You know, surely I can work that out for myself, can't I?'

ARTHUR SMITH

So it's time to head back to the office for the afternoon, and as it's a nice day, we might take a walk through the park. As we do so, we come across a group of Australian women sunbathing. One is wearing tiny shorts and a tight T-shirt with FCUK ME written across her breasts. Another has on a cutaway top with 'I would, would you?' written across it. Yet a third wears shorts with 'Slap here' written across the butt. I'm not making this up: this combination of interesting invitations was seen and carefully taken note of last summer.

'A little too carefully,' I can almost hear you saying. Guilty as charged.

Now for our generation of Grumpy Old Men this really is an area where we have problems. 'Oh, dear,' all the women respond, 'well, get over it.' And you're right, of course, we have to get over it, and we more or less have gotten over it, but bear with us a moment while we talk you through it. After all, you did ask us to 'talk about it'.

Most Grumpy Old Men were brought up in households where men went out to earn the money and women stayed at home, looked after the house, did the shopping and took care of the kids. If it wasn't like that – and my own mother had a job all the time I can remember – we still probably had an idea that this was the model. If women did go out to work, it was widely recognised that the housework and general family responsibilities also fell to them too. This was manifestly unfair, and the only thing that can be said in defence is that that's the way it had always been.

On the other side of the coin, we were also brought up to regard women as different and slightly strange beings. Women were generally thought to be more delicate creatures than we were, so we opened doors for them, we gave up our seats on crowded buses and trains for them, and we tried to do the heavy lifting. I'm not quite sure how this squares with the fact that we also let them scrub the floors, clean the windows, cook the meals, take care of the children, do the shopping and wash the dishes, while we paid the electricity bill and arranged the holidays, but that's just one of life's many confusions.

What was in no doubt was that the man was at the head of the family. Even in families where the woman was far and away, and very obviously, the stronger character, there was usually some deference to the male. We didn't make this up: we've been the head of the herd for thousands of years, hunter-gatherers, bringing back the food and generally being pampered for our trouble.

Then, all of a sudden, in just a twinkling of an eye, the whole history of the relationship between men and women was turned on its head. The aftermath of the war, when women had taken on all the jobs that we'd pretended were too difficult for them to do, and discovered that driving a bus was possible for women just as easily as it was for men; the advent of the birth-control pill, the free love, free sex and free-thinking of the 1960s all combined to produce a revolution. Suddenly women demanded the equality that we'd been denying them for aeons.

And it was fun. They burnt their bras – I was never quite sure why they regarded that as a sign of liberation because I for one had never gone to any trouble to keep them in them. Suddenly there were as many women in higher education as there were men. We got to hang out with them and it was all great.

Everything was going fine, but then came the difficult bit. Maybe it was because, having waited so long for their freedom, it was now not happening fast enough for some women. Maybe it was the boiling-over of resentment that had built up over decades. Whatever the reasons, the result was that a lot of women got angry. Suddenly, opening doors for women was potentially offensive. Giving up your seat for a woman was

potentially patronising. And certainly looking at their breasts, which had been our divine right since the Fall, was completely out of the question.

The idea was that women could wear any clothes, as revealing and provocative as they liked, but they were doing it to please themselves, not us. If we thought they might also be doing it to catch some attention from a man, that just went to show what paternalistic, sexist throwbacks we really were.

Now this presented us with a challenge. I mean it. I don't want to sound like too much of a wimp, but part of my upbringing involved trying my best not to give offence to anyone, men or women, by my personal behaviour. I sometimes used to wait for weeks and weeks before asking a girl out. Not because of a fear of rejection, though that too, but mostly because I didn't want to put them in the awkward position of having to say 'no'. A lot of us have tried hard to be 'new men', we really have, but for the life of us, when we meet a really attractive woman, with large breasts, a plunging neckline and clearly not wearing a bra, we have difficulty keeping our eyes fixed on theirs.

I mean, let's be honest, she's not really my type, but who amongst us can watch some of those early episodes of that stupid garden makeover show and not be looking at Charlie Dimmock's tits? It doesn't matter how 'new man' you are, how liberated, how unsexist, or whatever the expression is – you've got to be noticing her breasts. Now there are women around who find this offensive, and we men don't want to give offence. But in these circumstances, we just don't stand a chance.

However, difficult though it was, we were just getting used to the idea that women could wear whatever they liked, or however little they liked, and we weren't supposed to look, when along comes a set of women with none of these hang-ups whatsoever.

They've got very nice bodies – indeed, they go to a lot of trouble to ensure that they continue to have nice bodies – daily workouts, drinking hundreds of gallons of water, etc., and they like to show them off. So they wear very small T-shirts with FCUK ME written on the front. Which I think can only mean that, while we know that in no circumstances are we allowed to acquiesce to this apparent proposal, we may be allowed to look. Why write FCUK ME across your breasts if you aren't trying to draw attention to them?

Every day the television programmes that at one time carried news and, indeed, still call themselves *The News*, instead show pictures from this premiere or that award ceremony at which the women appear to compete with each other for the sparcity of their dresses, or the ingenious manner in which it's being kept on. Bits of tape and string here and there. Kylie is not just putting her bum on show, but, in case we've somehow missed it, sticking it directly into the camera lens. Janet Jackson is just cutting to the chase and showing us her left tit.

So what's the problem? The problem is that we're now so used to the idea that we can't look, that we don't look. And if we do look, our pleasure is marred by the fact that we think we shouldn't be looking. But now we seem to be allowed to look, as long as we don't ogle. But when is it OK and when isn't it OK? We're in a state of confusion. And it makes us grumpy. Grumpy, sad, festering old misanthropes who don't know which way is up.

We've just finished watching the news coverage of the Oscars, and I have to say that there seem to have been fewer women with huge areas of their bodies on show than usual. What they were revealing too much of, as usual, is how idiotic they are. This is another of the few areas where men tend to make complete and total knob-heads of themselves less frequently than women. Awards acceptance speeches.

I'm not sure where this started – I think they were always embarrassing – but the first one that sticks in my mind was that woman from *Mrs Doubtfire*, Sally Field's 'You really like me' speech. How is it that everyone on the planet knew that this was the most ridiculous, egregious, agonising vomit imaginable, but she did not?

Other recent corkers include Halle Berry's nonsense about 'women of colour' a couple of years ago. One strange-looking woman this year, whose name I don't know, nor what she was in, treated us to a near-hysterical and rather personal statement about how much she loved her mother. That's always nice, but I'm not sure why a billion people need to know it. Then she started fanning her own face with her hand – I'm never sure what that does for women – and said, 'And I'm not going to cry.'

(I pause here to report that someone in the office has just told me that this woman suffered some particularly awful personal tragedy in her earlier life, which of course makes me seem like a callous bastard for bringing it up, but I still don't quite understand why it's necessary to share this stuff with half the planet.)

The best thing is the cut-aways to the faces in the audience when this sort of stuff is going on. The camera pans across a sort of frieze from Madame Tussaud's, in which you quickly glimpse faces of people you felt sure have been dead for years. Certainly, they've had so much plastic surgery that their faces haven't moved for years. Some are clearly caught up in it and don't think there is anything odd about a person having some sort of breakdown in front of a worldwide audience in 52 countries. In other faces I believe I see a hint of pleasure that this rival is in the process of making a total sphincter of herself. In yet others – and I think I saw this in the cut-aways of Clint Eastwood this year – there is an expression of appalled disbelief, much as he used to do so well in *Dirty Harry* when the idiot boss made an idiot remark. 'Very stylish,' I think you can hear him saying.

Anyway the afternoon is wearing on. By this time I'm beginning to think maybe I've done a good day's work, and I'm wondering if I can slip off home before the traffic gets worse. A glance at the watch: it's too late because my journey home is going to coincide with the school run. I don't know what this is like where you live, but around where I live this has become such a self-parody that I can only hope that some of these people are laughing at themselves.

LITTLE DARLINGS

'People treat children as though there is something wrong with them because they're ignorant and small. They say, "I'm so worried about Alexander's development. I mean, he's got no grasp of bonded numbers, no concept of phonics, his hand-to-eye coordination is all over the place. I mean, goodness knows what he's going to be like when he's born."'

JEREMY HARDY

Try to drive down almost any suburban street at about 3.30 on a weekday afternoon and it's like the scene they left out of *Absolutely Fabulous* because it was too over the top. You can picture it as clearly as I can. Most of the cars are 4 x 4s. At the top of the league there are Toyota Land-Cruisers, Range Rovers, loads of those new Mercedes, Porsches and BMWs, Nissan Prairies, Isuzu Troopers, Chrysler Jeeps, Mitsubishi Shoguns, that sort of thing. Last time I went in one of these it was racing over the sand-dunes in searing temperatures in the desert in Dubai. Maybe you've done it – you feel absolutely bloody certain that the thing is going to tip over, but thankfully it never does. Anyway, that's the sort of thing they were built for. Not navigating the speed bumps down Prince of Wales Drive.

Next down are the sort of toy 4 x 4s, those odd little Hondas, crappy old Hyundais, Daihatsus, Mazdas. Now we're more into the territory of something that couldn't 4 x 4 its way out of a Fisons grow-bag, but still you are nice and high up, so it makes you feel important.

Next are all the estate cars – mostly those Mercedes that stretch from here to Pimlico – the front wheels are turning left at the traffic lights and the rear wheels are still back by the bus-stop. There are loads of Volvos and the occasional BMW.

Lastly – and this is confined to the one-child family – there are the sports cars: hundreds and hundreds of those little Mazdas, MGs, BMWs, Toyotas. And that's not to mention the occasional Lexus, which means the old man is a drug dealer.

Standing on the pavement next to the cars is Chloe's mum, just taking the opportunity for a quick exchange of drivel with Tiffany's mum, to find out if she is just as concerned as we are about Miss Brophy who's teaching Class 6. We can just about stand it that Miss Brophy looks a bit too sexy to be a primary school teacher and has a stud in her nose. What we can't stand is that she doesn't seem to be setting enough homework, and Chloe is falling behind where her brother William was at this stage. And what with the entrance exams for Tiffins coming up, we're really sure that they should be doing a lot more work. Sometimes Tiffany has as little as three hours' homework per night.

Meanwhile, the Chloes and Tiffanys and Williams are straining against being held captive by the outstretched hand and wanting to get home as fast as possible to watch *Home and Away*. These women are oblivious to the fact that their cars are parked along the side of the road for about three-quarters of a mile, ensuring that the through traffic is backed up halfway to Penzance.

So the journey home is almost as bad as the journey to work in the mornings, and by the time we get home the grump quotient is threatening to veer off the meter. What we like to do now is to slump down in a chair – like we haven't been sitting in one for the last two hours – have a nice glass of wine put into our hands, and have our loved one say, 'Good day, dear?' That's all she needs to say; probably best now to switch off altogether for about 20 minutes or so while we download.

About this bleeding numb-nuts who did a three-point turn in the middle of the Wandsworth one-way system and nearly killed a motorcyclist and four pedestrians. About the virus in the IT system at work. About the fact that developers are putting up a whole new estate of overpriced McMansions on the former school playing field at the bottom of the street. Or this new poster advertising perfume, which has a picture of a prostrate naked women looking as though she's just had sex, or is just about to have sex.

'That's Sophie Dahl, darling.'

'You mean that fat one? I don't think so.'

'She's lost a lot of weight.'

'I thought she was the one who celebrated how wonderful it was for women to be overweight.'

'She was – then she lost three stone.'

I glaze over and start watching the weather forecast. 'Look at her, waving her bloody arms about as usual.'

Now one thing that Grumpy Old Men require after a hard day of grumbling is a quiet evening. Gone are the days when we wanted to grab a bite to eat, change our clothes and then go down the pub or, worse still, round to someone's house to socialise. Weekdays in particular, we want to slob out, eat our food, have a couple of glasses of wine or beer, fall asleep on the sofa, be nudged awake and go to bed feeling like doggy's do-dos.

We look forward to weekends because we can do our various 'men in sheds' routines – usually something allowing us vicariously to revisit our youth in some way or another – fiddling with motorbikes, boats, fishing rods, that sort of thing. What we do not look forward to is the prospect that we may have to go out for the evening.

'Don't forget we're going to Reg and Paula's on Saturday.'

'Who the bloody hell are Reg and Paula?'

Reg and Paula, it turns out, are having a party. You'd rather power-sand your own backside than go, but there's no choice and you're going. Now for most of my life I feel I've known what a party is. A party is where you invite all your real mates and nobody you don't really like but who could be good for your career. You tell them it's casual dress, and they all turn up in their jeans, idiot T-shirts and Reeboks. You calculate how many people the available space can hold, and then invite that number plus about 20 more. You buy enormous quantities of wine, of fairly indifferent quality, and about 100 bottles of beer – or, if you really are in a desperate post-student phase, some of those Party 7s.

People bring a bottle of red wine and then drink white. Actually, it's the same bottle of red that you took to their place three months ago. You buy a whole load of food, quite a lot of it from Marks & Spencer – long sticks of French bread, loads of cheese and pâté, crisps, nuts, sausage rolls, all good, cheap and rubbishy. You roll the carpets up and push the furniture back in one room, and set up the hi-fi.

It is, these days, imperative that no one under the age of 35 is present because they would spoil everyone's evening by sneering at your music collection and being openly appalled by the dancing. What you want is a whole lot of Tamla Motown so that once drink has been taken, the women can line up and do their impressions of the Supremes. Loads of Stones – so that when they are good and drunk your fatter mates can give everybody a great laugh with their legendary Mick Jagger impressions and everybody else can join in with the 'I said yeah, yeah, yeah, whooo'. You want a few Status Quo tracks for the air-guitar heroes. You need 'All Right Now' and maybe a bit of Hot Chocolate doing 'You Sexy Thing' for our younger viewers.

Everyone has too much to drink and dances ludicrously until they are a frenzy of sweat. Windows are thrown open even in freezing weather, and there is a strong chance that the neighbours will call the police. Everyone came with a clear determination to keep a clear head, but somewhere along the line they decided 'Sod it' and got into some serious drinking and now have to get cabs or stagger home. At about one in the morning people start to trickle away. They make too much noise shouting goodbye in the street, and you do a bit of gentle shushing as you see the neighbours' bedroom lights go on. When you wake up in the morning you find someone sleeping under the sofa.

Now that's what I call a party.

What do people like Reg and Paula call a party? You drive around the block ten times because it's residents' parking for a 5-mile radius, and then sit in the car for ten minutes because you can't arrive less than half an hour after the invitation time. You find the house and walk down the path, but when you get to the front door there is no noise or other sign of life, so you have to walk back to get under the light from the street-lamp to check the address on the invitation. You find that it is the right house, and you knock on the door. It's answered by a man wearing a Blue Harbour rugby shirt with a number on the chest, chinos and trainers. He looks quizzically for a moment and then says, 'Oh, you must be… [whoever you are]. You're friends of Paula, aren't you? Do come in and meet everybody.'

You go into the living room to find a row of people you've never met before standing in a semi-circle, all with a glass of white wine in their hands. All the men are bald on top, and most have got very closely cropped hair at the sides. They're all wearing Blue Harbour. All the women are in various stages of retreat from the Marianne Faithfull hairstyle and colour, and all are wearing trouser suits that make them look as though they've just been to a meeting of the parent-teachers association, or, if they're feeling really bohemian, they might have on a nice Laura Ashley print.

You are introduced. 'This is Philip, he's an investment banker; this is his wife Rosemary. This is – sorry I didn't catch your name. Yes, this is Jonathan, he's an architect; this is his wife Pauline. This is Michael, he's a lawyer; and this is his wife Moira. Michael and Moira live next door, so they won't have far to stagger home.' Everyone laughs politely. 'This is Frank, he's my bank manager, so be nice to him…' Everyone laughs a little bit more, '…and Frank's wife, also called Pauline, so don't get confused. And this is Anthony, who is our local vicar. We call him St Anthony.' Now we're laughing so uproariously that we're in danger of involuntary leakage. 'This is James…this is Harry…this is Martha…' It's all faded into a blur because by now you wish you were dead.

'There are two more couples coming later; I think you might know the Meldrews, and the Cathcarts said they're going to be late because they've got to pop in on the Fitzroy-Wagners, who are also having a party tonight, but we didn't know. Now then, what can I get you to drink?'

So this is it, then. This is a party 21st-century style, and this prat has invited his neighbours, his bank manager and his vicar. We're going to drink no more than two glasses of Pouilly Fuissé that they brought back last time they took the ferry to Calais because it was an absolute steal at 5 euros a bottle. Meanwhile, Ron and Paula's two 12-year-old daughters do a continuous circulation with vol-au-vents. They've obviously been bribed, probably with a new pony.

No salmon and cream cheese whirls from M & S for Ron and Paula. Not for them those flaky pastry parcels filled with hot mushroom soup that sticks to the roof of your mouth causing a serious scald. No mini-sausage rolls or cut-up pieces of scotch egg. No, we're having little pieces of sushi. Tiny pastry tarts containing a little swirl of pâté inserted with an icing nozzle. And for a special treat later on, a warmed-up bite-size burger.

We're going to stand around talking about the congestion charge and listen to people explain how their children were too gifted to go to the local comprehensive, so regrettably they have to drive them halfway across London to go to the private school where the new headmaster is doing wonders. We're going to talk about cricket and Jonny Wilkinson's magical kick and how it was almost as though it was in slow motion. We're going to be sorry to have to say it, but the asylum seekers situation has got totally out of hand. I was stopped on the high street last week by a woman carrying a baby and with a notice saying she was from Kosovo, but she didn't look like she was from Kosovo to me. And nobody is going to ask, 'Why didn't she leave her baby in the Kosovo refugees' crèche?' We're going to be asked, 'And what do you do?' followed by 'That must be interesting', and we're going to ask the same questions in return. And any time from about 10 p.m. onwards I'm going to be trying to catch my wife's eye so that I can tap my watch. She, meanwhile, is studiously avoiding catching my eye because it's far too early to leave without seeming rude. However, I don't really care about seeming rude because I'd rather split open my own tongue with a rusty scythe than spend another two minutes in the company of these tossers.

'Well, you could have made an effort,' I'm told on the way home.

'I did make an effort, but if I had to listen to one more description of the route Michael chooses to drive on his way to their house in the Cotswolds I would have eaten my own head. And I thought you said there was going to be food. I'm starving.'

'There was food. Paula spent most of the last three days preparing it.'

'I wonder if the McDonalds is still open. I could murder a Big Mac.' It is. We do. We wish we hadn't. A perfect end to a perfect evening.

THE PERILS OF GOING OUT

'What I hate in restaurants is waiters who say,
"Have you eaten here before? Let me explain our
concept." And you say, "No, no, before you start, let
me explain. My concept is this dinner, it's my dinner
and I'm hungry. That's my concept. Now do you
think you can get your servile little body around
that concept?"'

A. A. GILL

Actually, eating out generally is something else that has turned
from being a relative pleasure to a bloody provocation from
beginning to end. And this is all very recent, isn't it? Does it
date from the age of the 'celebrity chef' and the whole new
extraordinary snobbery there is about the number of Michelin
stars, or the amount of abuse the restaurant has had from the
poison pen of Michael Winner? It used to be very
straightforward. There was a restaurant in the local high street
run by someone called Giovanni who made a very good
cannelloni. A bottle of cheap plonk, a few breadsticks and
you'd be in and out for about 12 quid a head. Nice meal. No
poncing about. A quick nosebag and then home.

What is it now? They're all run by people off the telly –
made famous by their very odd haircuts or their willingness to
charge you a breathtaking amount of money for a mushroom.
If you are stupid enough to want to go to one of those
ridiculous places, and you aren't fortunate enough to have a
familiar-sounding surname, such as Bragg or Dimbleby, you're
unlikely to be able to book a table at all. If you happen to call
up and catch them at a weak moment, you might be able to
book a table for a special occasion next August, and then only if

you are willing to turn up by 7 p.m. and promise to vacate the table by 9.30 so they can clear up for the second sitting.

When you arrive they take your coat and check on your tailoring. If you are dressed in anything less than Jasper Conran, they look at you as though you've just crawled out of the sewers of Rio de Janeiro.

'Oh, yes, sir, you're the first to arrive,' as though even that's a crime. 'Do you want a drink in the bar or will you go to the table?'

Now I don't usually drink more than a bottle of wine with my dinner, so I want to order it straight away and have the first glass while I'm consulting the menu, but that causes mayhem, and robs them of the chance to sell me a gin and tonic for £15.

'May I get you some water for the table?' What are they talking about? Does the table need watering? 'Still or sparkling?' Even after all this time I can't get used to this. 'Gently carbonated' it says on the label. Gently carbonated? What on earth does that mean? Is it their way of saying it's got a gentle fizz but it's not an Alka-Seltzer? Gently carbonated? Give me strength.

'Still, please,' and what you actually want is tap water, but you have to be an especially robust personality to say so. What it comes down to is that you would rather pay as much for a glass of bottled water as you would for a glass of decent wine than risk the embarrassment of asking for what you actually want. Tap water, with fewer impurities in it these days than the bottled water you are paying through the nose for. Have we totally taken leave of our senses?

They give you a menu written in French and in what we are presumably supposed to believe is the chef's or the maître d's handwriting. Now why do they do that? What is the point they are trying to make by writing menus in French? You wouldn't write it in Thai in a Thai restaurant, would you? Or Urdu in an

Indian? No, the point is very simple – it's a reinforcement of the British class system, which is designed to make you feel inadequate if you haven't had the benefit of a 'proper' education.

What else could it be for? It's not like enjoying opera better in the original Italian is it? You don't enjoy the food more because you've ordered it in French? If you are lucky enough to have had a decent start in life, this probably won't have occurred to you at all as a problem; but take it from me, every week thousands of people sit in pretentious restaurants all over Britain squinting at these daft bloody menus, unwilling to let on that they don't know what the hell it is they are ordering, hoping that no one will ask them, and end up eating octopus or something else with suckers on it when what they really wanted was a prawn cocktail.

Happily, when I went to school you pretty much had to learn some French, and, anyway, if I don't understand it, I just ask the waiter, 'What the fuck is that?' Or I pick the snobbiest person in the company and ask them – you'd be surprised how often they don't know either. But lots of people don't do this. They are just made to feel like something the waiter wiped off his shoe because they didn't have the same privileged education as all the fat pompous bastards surrounding them in the restaurant.

And in the unlikely event that you can understand it, what does it say when translated? It says, 'Corn-fed and hand-reared Cornish chicken that has luxuriated in warm baths and enjoyed gentle rub-downs each day until it was allowed to choose its own method of death, and then lovingly hand-plucked by happy peasants, marinated for three weeks in a consommé of pure egg yolk, truffle, marjoram and butter made from the milk of wild goats from the foot of the Andes. Then it is lightly broiled in a pan made out of copper which was mined using well-paid local labour from Zambia, and then tossed with a mixture of herbs and spices first discovered by Marco Polo...' Well, of course I could go on and on...and if you think I'm exaggerating, treat yourself to lunch at the River Café.

Anyway, the plate comes and someone has drizzled a pattern of a red sticky liquid all around the edges and the quantity of food is usually in inverse proportion to the price. By this time you are starving, so it's gone in about three and a half minutes.

Now if, when I was a small boy – and my mother used to feed a family of four on £5 a week and worry what to give us on Thursday because my dad got paid on Friday – if at that time someone had told me that I would be willing to pay £17 for a piece of steak about the diameter of a golf ball, I'd have asked, 'Has there been a nuclear holocaust?' But here we are. It's the 21st century and this is what passes for entertainment.

So, being a man who likes a quiet life, I sometimes suggest going out without the bother of actually having to talk to anyone. To the cinema.

Do you remember when one of the simple pleasures of life was going to the pictures? When we were very small we used to go to the Regal in West Norwood. We'd see a short B-feature, although I didn't know it was called a B-feature, then a lot of advertisements and 'Sunday for seven days' and finally the A-feature. Sometimes it would be something epic, such as *Ben Hur* or *Spartacus* or *The Alamo* or *The Guns of Navarone*. Truly great films, where you strode out of the cinema thinking you were Yul Brynner or Steve McQueen, and were bloody sure you'd had your money's worth.

Then, a bit later, we would go to the Savoy in Heaton Moor High Street. In those days it was a good old-fashioned flea-pit. You'd buy some of that watery orange juice, Kia-ora (what does that mean?), and maybe some popcorn and go in to see *The Sting* or *Butch Cassidy and the Sundance Kid* or *The Graduate* or *Midnight Cowboy*. Certainly there would be a couple of advertisements for the local Chinese restaurant or scrap-metal dealers, but nothing to make you shuffle in your seats.

What's it like today? You have to phone them in advance and speak the name of your local cinema into a recorded device. You find yourself enunciating 'Salisbury New Canal' in your best English, and hear their digital recording say, 'I think you said "Salisbury New Canal". Press the star button now if this is correct.' You do. Then you are locked into a duel with technology in which you have to position your fingers carefully over the buttons on the handset, and respond with speed and dexterity to the instructions given. '*The Sweet Sins of Sexy Susan*, certificate PG, press 2 for showing times, or 3 to move to the next film.' You press 3. The recording is halfway through the title of the next film and you didn't quite catch it. Which button do you press to have it repeated? And how do you manage to keep your fingers on the right buttons while writing down what they're saying? Momentary confusion is enough to throw the whole process into mayhem, and before you know where you are, you're back at the start or, worse still, hearing 'Thank you, please call again' and a terminating click.

Can you imagine a grumpy in charge of an F16 fighter bomber trying to choose in a split second between Iraqi or Allied tanks on the ground at a crossroads 500 feet below you? Now that would make the expression 'friendly fire' even more sick than it already is.

So let's cut to the chase and fantasise that you've managed to order your tickets on the phone or net, and you turn up at the cinema. It's a nightmare of neon in blue and yellow, with hundreds of people in a maze of corridors, all funnelling through a food hall with more artificial flavourings and colourings and E-numbers per square inch than anywhere else on earth. No colour or smell found there occurs in nature. There was more fresh food on the unmanned mission to Mars than there is in this place. And have you ever wondered why cinemas don't confine themselves to selling food items in wrappers that don't make a noise when you open them? Just think of the sum total of human misery that could have been avoided over the years by such a simple measure.

So while you are queuing to have your ticket torn up by an obnoxious youth with tattoos, you watch fat people with fat children buying a barrel of popcorn, a foul-smelling hotdog with layers of mustard and ketchup, and – this is the killer – a bucket of Diet Coke. There's about 200,000 calories in the food, and they insist that the sugary drink is 'diet' – doesn't it slay you? And finally you are in.

The cinema is about the size of your living room, with a screen about 50 per cent larger than the TV you bought last

Christmas. You look at your watch. It's 7.20, exactly the time you were told the programme was going to start. To be fair, it starts on time, but what does it start with?

A film showing a demonic-looking man heating up a branding iron that he looks ready to ram into your butt. This short film is about piracy, and urges us not to help the pirates by buying knocked-off stuff. Now we don't mind this in principle – but what we don't want is to have the piss taken out of us. 'The pirates are out to get you,' says the voice of God. Well, not really; it seems to me that they are out to get *you*. What they're offering *me* seems to be a cheap version of the stuff you've been overcharging me for these last 40 years. Anyway, I'm a captive audience, you have my attention, what else? 'Piracy affects us all.' Does it? Not really; I can see how it affects you, but it's a bit of a stretch to see how it affects me. Yes, eventually you are going to make less money and invest in fewer movies, but somehow I think you are going to survive it. 'Piracy funds organised crime.' Now steady on – are you trying to imply that if I buy a knocked-off video at the local street-market I'm funding the sex-slave trade? But they haven't finished yet. 'Piracy supports terrorism.' OK, so now you want us to believe that the blokes who flew their planes into the twin towers got their funding from replica CDs of Beyoncé on sale in Petticoat Lane?

Is your reaction to this the same as mine? I was prepared to be sympathetic to the idea of not buying knocked-off stuff if they just asked me nicely, but now you can fuck off. Right after the end of the movie I'm going out looking for a dodgy dealer with a branding iron. And then, at the very end, and this really is adding insult to injury, they say, 'Thank you for listening.' Like I had a choice. That's the funny thing about your ears: unless you actually stick your fingers in them, they're open. If I'm sitting here waiting for the film to start, I'm listening.

If I'd had any say in it, I wouldn't have listened. If it had been up to me, we would have got straight on with the film. So give me all this bollocks if you insist on it, but don't then thank me for listening. OK?

So I sit through that, and next we see the Carlton Screen Advertising trailer. OK, I guess it's a fair cop; I'm a captive audience and, even though I am paying to sit here rather than being paid to do so, the cinema is going to sell my eyeballs and attention to an advertiser. What's it going to be? An Indian man bashing his old car into the shape of a new one. OK, probably a bit patronising, but mildly amusing. Go on. Gordon's gin. Yes, yes, I never buy the stuff, but the ad is reasonably well shot, so I can put up with it. I seem to have grown up to the tune of 'Any time, any place, anywhere', so I'm well used to sitting through advertisements for drinks I'd never touch unless I was in the Gobi Desert and this was the only liquid refreshment for 200 miles.

The next seems to be for a small screen of some kind, which you hold in your hand and which may be a mobile phone, and now I'm getting into difficult territory. I used to know what a mobile phone does: it makes phone calls without wires. Quite handy. Nowadays I'm not sure. The latest advertisement has a businessman obviously in some foreign hotel, staring at this small screen and being told by his wife at home that she 'can't put it all in', and attracting the attention of some lascivious-looking Japanese next to him. What they basically seem to be implying is that this phone is a way of sending pornographic messages.

Elsewhere I'm informed that it's 'Bluetooth at 10 metres'. Now the advertisers don't even think I know what this means. They've simply decided that I and my generation of grumpies aren't part of their target market, so it doesn't really matter if part of their message goes winging right over the top of our heads. And that's all right, but if you don't really care if I understand your ad or not, then put the stinking thing on MTV, or Nickelodeon, or whatever noisy and sex-ridden channel your target audience watches. Don't waste my time sticking it in front of the audience for *Lost in Translation* – a totally crap film, but mentioned in this context because it seems to have been watched exclusively by 50-year-old couples who wished they hadn't bothered, and certainly have not the smallest idea of what 'Bluetooth at 10 metres' means.

So we sit through all these ads, not knowing where one ends and the next begins, and at last, when you think there is nothing more to oppress you with, you hear a mobile going off in the back of the auditorium. You are ready to be irritated beyond endurance when you hear another one going off somewhere else, and then another, and it turns out to be a reminder to turn your mobile off. Thank you. Very good joke. Can we get on now?

Then you hear an earthquake at the back of the cinema and a racing car going around the perimeter, just to give you the vitally important information that you are listening in Sensurround or Surroundsound or something designed to make you think you're going to be run over in the car chase.

And if that's not bad enough, we're then going to be subjected to a load of film trailers that some dork has deemed suitable for showing to this audience. So we're treated to a series of noisy and grisly sequences of people turning into androids and then into machines with super-human strength and x-ray vision, who are determined to take over the Earth by violent means and which I wouldn't go to see even if Cindy Crawford were going to perform an intimate personal service on me after I'd sat through it. (Well, on reflection, I might in those circumstances, but since that's not very likely, we probably don't have to worry about it.)

Finally, when your arse is already getting numb from sitting in the same place for such a long time with your knees under your chin, and when you have just about lost consciousness with boredom, the screen dissolves into a mêlée of bubbles and squiggles and eventually resolves into some small print that informs you that Odeon is 'Fanatical about Film'. No they're not; they're fanatical about getting you into the cinema and finding ever more ingenious ways of getting money out of you. And even if they were, who gives a flying fart what they are fanatical about? You are going to come back to the cinema if it's warm and comfortable and you can find a place to park, and they're showing a film you want to see, and you are still awake by the time it starts. In no circumstances are you going to return to the cinema because they are 'fanatical about film'. That's another 15 seconds of my life that I'm never going to get back.

No, the truth is that there is so much about going out that makes me grumpy that I'm truly best off staying in. That way I can sit on my own settee, with my feet on my own pouffe, a glass of my own wine in my hand and grumble about whatever is on the telly.

SMALL-SCREEN ANGST

'I put on the news and discovered that they took Trevor McDonald's desk away. He's just standing there, and you think, "What's that all about?" And gradually it dawns on you that somebody must have said, "I've got an idea that will really make the news-viewing experience much improved — we'll take your desk away." How do they possibly see this sort of thing as an improvement?'

BILL BRYSON

Perhaps more than anything else, the telly is a source of renewable energy as far as irritation is concerned. And that's because it is, of course, all getting worse. It's the place where so many of the things that piss us off come together. It's the melting pot of news, youth culture, runaway deviant sex, weather forecasters, ridiculous game shows, and people forever trying to ingratiate themselves with us in some way or other.

Take for example the new super-duper set for *ITV News*. Visualise it in your mind for a moment – it's like something between one of those wraparound 3D cinema screens that makes you feel you're falling over the edge of a cliff and a Paris fashion show. A great semi-circular screen at the back and a catwalk in the front.

ITV spent about £1 million on this nonsense. £1 million and, as most people know, there isn't actually anything there at all in real life. Just a little pathway for the newsreaders to walk along and everything else is 'virtual', which I think is just an expensive way of saying 'it doesn't exist'.

All you can think of when you're watching the introduction to every story is how they've choreographed the walk, and the changing pictures in the background, to look as cool and 'Hey, wow' as they can, rather than whether the thing

is really going to make sense. Newsreaders have to walk
sideways, looking at the camera, so they can reveal the
changing images on the screen behind them. Poor old Sir
Trevor, a thoroughly decent man with some old-fashioned
journalistic instincts, looks about as comfortable as I would
dressed like a Bay City Roller. Can you imagine old Alastair
Burnett doing that? Or Reginald Bosanquet? Remember him?
It was all he could do to keep his toupée on straight, let alone
walk sideways while talking. Now that's what I call a
newsreader. No, the whole thing is yet another major step
further in the trend towards form over content: it looks
fabulous, but does it have anything to do with the news?

So after this little ballet in the studio, we're about to come
to the news report itself. At one time it used to be OK to say
'Kate Adie reports'. That got a bit boring, so they used to vary it
with 'Jeremy Bowen has this report' or 'Julian Mannion sends
this report'. Stage three was a little more adventurous; it might
be 'James Mates has been following the days events', or has
been 'tracing the run-up to…'. This week I heard that the
economics correspondent 'has been reflecting on the
circumstances that led to…'. Oh, has he? A little light
reflection? How nice for him.

Then, when we get into a few pictures from the scene and
just in case we can't remember what we heard six seconds ago,
there's a little logo on the screen saying 'BIG BROTHER
ESCAPE', or 'FOOTBALLERS' WIVES'. We cut to the hapless sod
in the middle of nowhere relevant, who tells us mostly what
we've just heard in the studio but with a few more pictures and
utterly meaningless interviews – sometimes as much as ten
words long. He or she 'signs off' with a sincere look into the
camera, and then once we're back in the studio we find that the
reporter is still 'live at the scene', so the newsreader looks up at
a non-existent screen and asks him or her three scripted

questions that may or may not elaborate slightly more on what we've just heard.

This is a living demonstration of the old adage of television journalists everywhere: 'Tell them what you are going to tell them, tell them, and then tell them what you've told them.' Well, why not? We're all stupid enough to sit there watching, so we deserve to be treated like morons.

REALITY SUCKS

'Fair play to Carol Vorderman, but I thought that when Jeffrey Archer came out of prison she'd be running up to him with a microphone and they'd rush to Thames Studios and do a fund-raising charity thing called "Personality Disorders".'

JEREMY HARDY

We can't go through the whole schedule picking out every irritant that gets up our noses because there aren't enough tissues in the world to cope with the sneezing. On the other hand, I don't think we'd be doing our duty if we didn't have a few nasty words on the side for the most recent wave of what I believe is called 'reality TV', even though thankfully it's about as far from my reality as the wise and literate president in *The West Wing* is from the president who sent troops into Baghdad.

I was talking about this to a friend of mine recently, whose name I won't mention because it would sound as though I was 'dropping'. Suffice it to say that he's on the telly a lot. He told me that last time *Big Brother* was on the TV he walked into the living room of his house to find his wife and two sons watching a man iron a shirt. He stood there watching them watch the man ironing the shirt, and it went on and on and on.

'Why are you all sitting here watching a man iron a shirt?'
There was no reply. 'At least iron a shirt. That way, at the end of
it, you've got an ironed shirt.'

'Shhh, Dad, something might be going to happen.'

Well, it might be going to happen, sure, but in the event,
it doesn't. What actually happens is that nothing happens.
A bunch of total airheads slob around for simply hours and
hours and hours on end, showing off as much of their variously
attractive or otherwise bodies as they can, with nothing
worthwhile to do, and nothing worthwhile to say, and we all sit
and watch them doing it. Eight, is it? Eight or a dozen young
people spend however much time it is in each other's company,
and never, so far as we can tell, have a conversation about the
war in Iraq, the environment, the use of energy, Third World
debt, AIDS in Africa, euthanasia, abortion, GM crops, student
loans, God, death… I could go on and on and no doubt I do.

If we had been put into that situation aged 18–25, we
would have solved the whole world's problems by the time
we'd come out. Instead we learn that Jade may or may not have
given a blow-job to that bloke with the shaved head, and that

anybody who accidentally stumbles into the house carrying the Dingle family brain-cell finds a way to bust out. And we don't even have an ironed shirt.

In the *Grumpy Old Men* series, Will Self described this as the *circus maximus* of a decadent culture. Undoubtedly that's right; but as time goes on it seems to me to be more like the equivalent of the old Bedlam asylum, which members of the privileged classes would visit on a Sunday afternoon to watch the lunatics throwing themselves around or eating their own fingers. Increasingly, it seems to me that we are watching various misfits and, worse still, people with genuine psychological problems unravel in front of our eyes. What these people plainly need is professional help of some sort, rather than to be encouraged to exacerbate their problems still further by having their private matters so publicly examined – first on the television in front of an audience of voyeurs, and then via the newspapers which, on this one occasion, don't even need an excuse to delve as far as the mood takes them into people's most intimate personal lives.

But you know, it's not all that easy for the commissioning editors. For every one of these things that captures the public imagination, there is extra pressure on the people who commission programmes to come up with variations on the theme. And, surprise surprise, the next step is usually more extreme, or even further down-market. And thus *Neighbours from Hell* begets everything else you can think of 'from hell'. *Blind Date* eventually begets *There's something about Miriam*. The latest commission, I read today, is called *Going to Work Naked*.

The total acreage of desert that stretches before us across 200 channels every night is enough to fuel several volumes of grumpy ranting, by the end of which we'd all have thrown the noose over the rafters, popped in our heads and kicked away the stool. So let's be brief. The frequently uttered warning that 'more means worse' has undoubtedly come true. There is still a lot of great stuff on the telly, but it is harder and harder to find. Meanwhile, the worst stuff is so much worse that just when you think you have reached the point where you are unshockable, you see Graham Norton simulating receiving a homosexual blow-job, or a set of sad inadequates feeling each other up in a mud-bath. How much worse can it get after that? Just keep watching.

A few years ago Rupert Murdoch gave the prestigious McTaggart Lecture at the Edinburgh Television Festival. That in itself was a bit like putting Slobodan Milosovic in charge of the war crimes trial at The Hague. In it he accused the television community of being a load of snobs making programmes for each other that perpetuated the class system by looking backwards to a world we used to love rather than forwards to the world he was creating. I think he meant programmes like *Jewel in the Crown*, *Brideshead Revisited*, *The Forsyte Saga* and *Pride and Prejudice*. Well, congratulations, Rupe. We ain't going to see much of that any more. No sirree. We're going to see *I'm a Celebrity, Get Me out of Here* and read in the papers that the boss of ITV is reported to have referred to it as public service broadcasting. Which, of course, cannot possibly be accurate.

BEDTIME FOR GRUMPY

'Just because some bird came out of a nightclub and got into a car and a bloke with a camera was really low down and saw that she wasn't wearing any knickers, now she's on Pop Idol, and the next thing you know she's on The Game, jumping over hurdles.'

JEREMY CLARKSON

So now it's getting close to our bedtime. Being insomniacs, Grumpy Old Men have to go to bed relatively early if we are to get any sleep at all. We've tried just about everything you can think of to induce a long sleep. We've tried drinking lots of wine, and not drinking lots of wine, and drinking a moderate amount of wine. We've tried not eating for a few hours before we go to bed, and occasionally we've tried a hot milky drink – though that makes us feel too much like our grandmas. We've tried a warm bath, a cold room, a warm room. Good heavens,

we've even occasionally tried consensual sex – a revolting thought for our younger readers, I know, but hey, we're trying to be honest here.

Nothing works. We go off to sleep fast enough usually, but then somewhere between midnight and 3 a.m. we're wide awake. We turn over and see those little red numbers flashing in the darkness. Turn over again and try to empty our minds. Turn over again because it's filling up at the speed of an upturned car in a river with all the bloody irritations that seem to be raining down on us from everywhere we look. No, too late. Our minds are full of hundreds of our little demons, who are prodding us and laughing at us and making us wonder what in the name of all that is holy it is all about. Why do we bother? Why not pack it all in...?

Time to remember. Quick. Everything I think at three in the morning must be bollocks. Turn over again. Turn on the radio. Oh good, it's *Westway*.

CHAPTER 5

Special occasions

So now, having dealt at laborious and tedious length with what our daily lives are like on a more or less average day, you might expect the monotony of being a Grumpy Old Man to be broken up by those events that your wife or partner carefully marks out in the calendar – birthdays, mother's day, anniversaries, that sort of stuff.

Although this is one area where there is a lot of divergence in the views of various Grumpy Old Men, depending on their time of life, the time of life of their kids, etc., I think it's fair to say that the genuine Grumpy Old Man would probably, when all things are considered, prefer the year to be totally devoid of any so-called 'special occasions' whatever.

Yes, I know this sounds as though it goes beyond the bounds of average grumpiness and tiptoes alarmingly into misanthropy, but we might as well face it. Whereas of course we do occasionally get some genuine pleasure out of little moments or aspects of birthdays, father's day, mother's day, Christmas and so forth, the inescapable fact is that the surrounding nonsense of them all, and the utter bollocks of some of them, make it what I think some people call a zero-sum game. Put more clearly, that means the downside outweighs the upside. Put more clearly still, the crap weighs more heavily than the joy.

So whereas, for example, Christmas in some ways provides a welcome break from work and daily routine, and, depending on the age of our kids, we generally quite like to see our loved ones enjoying themselves, in the end the short list of good things about Christmas just doesn't compensate for all the bullshit. And that's because the pleasure of seeing your kids opening their presents lasts about ten minutes, as does the pleasure of sitting down to Christmas lunch, until the moment you start to feel serious empathy for the stuffed turkey. Meanwhile, all the accompanying crapulence lasts, in various degrees of intensity, from September to January.

Several of the grumpy contributors to the *Grumpy Old Men at Christmas* programme made what I thought was the very sensible suggestion that there should be a law that forbids anyone from mentioning Christmas until, say – well, John Sergeant thought about 20 December. That seems about right to me.

This isn't as grumpy as it sounds because the theory goes that a shorter period of relatively intense (for some) excitement and pleasure is better than weeks and weeks of fake festivities and crappy tinsel and execrable Christmas lights and sodding Slade or bloody Roy Wood chanting their tinny drivel everywhere you go. If the preparations just went on for a few days instead of a few months, we wouldn't feel so dreadfully weary and sick to death of the whole ridiculous nonsense by the time it arrives. And if there wasn't such an extended period of supposed 'climax', the inevitable anti-climax would be less desperate than it currently undoubtedly is.

Three days of build-up – trees are bought and erected, decorations go up, idiots can put as many inflatable Santas climbing their roofs as they like, you do your shopping, get a bit of extra food and drink in, and then totally slob out for three or four days. Then it all comes down and sanity recommences. That's what I would call a good Christmas. Well, that would at least be an OK Christmas.

Why can't we do this here? Other countries, so far as I can see, don't start counting the shopping days to Christmas on 1 September. Even the USA, which God knows is far more barking than we are in almost any way you can think of, makes much less fuss about Christmas than we do. I know, I know, they do Thanksgiving, but even that isn't a shadow of the collective insanity that seems to grip us.

No, it's times like Christmas that are guaranteed to bring out the grump in most Grumpy Old Men. Almost everything about it seems destined to nauseate us. From start to finish it is its own litany of flesh-creeping irritations.

Carol singers. Tuneless, snotty-nosed kids who sing half a line and then stick their hands out to relieve you of cash. This starts in October and goes on to Christmas Eve, and if you short-change them, you're likely to get a festive greeting spray-painted on the side of your car.

Nativity plays. Someone else's kid is always Joseph or the Virgin Mary, and yours is always part of the 'chorus' and standing at the back so you can't see them. Instead you get to see hours and hours of the usual hyper-parented little brats, who are obviously the apples of the teacher's eye, hogging the limelight, with their god-awful grandparents 'oohing' and 'aahing' and leaning across you with their state of the art digital camera to record the event for posterity.

Christmas trees. Half the forests of the world are hacked down and ranged across every pavement as you're trying to walk past, so you slip on the needles and come perilously close to dropping your carrier bag full of bottles of Advocaat or Bailey's on to the hard pavement. By the time you're ready to buy your tree, all the decent ones are gone, and any stragglers that remain are about to shed their needles, usually on the way back to your car.

Buying presents. Now this is a really challenging area for the average grumpy, and I have to confess that I still haven't quite found the best way to handle it. In the early days I used to try, I really did, to buy something for my wife that she might genuinely want to receive. I'd go as far as to look at some of the jewellery, handbags, perfume and even clothes she had bought herself recently to get an idea of the kind of thing she would like. Yep, I tried. Then I'd resign myself to what, for me, would be an absolute marathon shopping session, sometimes as much as an hour and a half.

Over a period of a few years I've bought bits and pieces of jewellery, pullovers, perfume, books, videos and, yes, once I even bought a dress. And to be fair, on Christmas morning itself I've been made to believe that I have chosen well. She will go through all the right 'I wonder what it can be' noises as she's opening it. She'll say, 'What lovely wrapping paper' as it's coming off. She'll pause just before the final revelation to add extra poignancy to the moment. Then she'll say, 'That's wonderful' in tones that not even the CIA's most sophisticated expert lie-detector would reveal as anything less than totally sincere.

And it doesn't stop there. From time to time during the day she'll review what I have bought her, do a bit more 'oohing' and 'aahing' and then I'll never see the item again. Actually, that's not quite true: one time, about ten years after I'd bought it, I recognised the dress I'd chosen among the stuff that was going out to the charity shop.

So anyway, after a few years of this we came to an accommodation. My wife would buy her own Christmas presents. And she does – so that on Christmas Eve I'm ceremonially handed a few carrier bags full of items – little books with hand-sewn covers to make little notes in, little lacquered boxes too small to put anything in, the odd item of clothing, a scented candle of some description – stuff that I never ever could have chosen in a month of trying. The following morning we go through a strange ritual of me handing her presents, and her opening the wrapping I've hastily bundled them into and half-pretending to be surprised.

For much the same reason that buying presents for your wife or partner is a disaster, it's also a mistake for a grumpy to try to buy presents for everyone else. First, you've probably got to be in a good mood to buy presents wisely, and by definition this cannot be the case. You're out shopping, so how can you be in a good mood? Second, grumps genuinely don't have the slightest idea what people will want, so they end up buying something they would like to receive themselves. And that simply doubles the problem: the person who receives it doesn't want it, and the person you gave it to now has something you want yourself, which just makes you want it more.

And then there is the whole question of receiving presents yourself. I'm constantly told that I am 'difficult to buy for', and I don't sense that this is in 'what do you buy for the man who has everything' territory. It's more in the 'what do you buy for the man who can't really be arsed to want anything' area. This is the syndrome that has led to that most eccentric and English of habits – that of buying socks. What a very strange thing to do, and what a triumph for the sock marketing board, or whatever it is. Because what could possibly be less festive than socks for Christmas? I was going to say underpants, but then I recall that I have in fact received my share of underpants at Christmas, and it does indeed provide marginally more festive fare than socks.

More eccentric even than that, in a way, is ties. Now a tie

for a man is a very personal statement, and you are very unlikely to get him one that he actually likes. But how about getting him a tie with a bloody great picture of a snowman emblazoned across it and which, when you press the snowman's nose, plays a synthesised version of the music from *The Snowman* animation. Exactly how often are you going to wear that, I wonder?

So because everyone knows I am a miserable old sod, they usually buy me books. Books about motorbikes because I ride a motorbike. (I also sometimes get the bus, but I don't want to read a book about buses.) Books about movies. (I like watching films but have very little interest in reading about them.) Books about Eric Clapton. (I'm a big fan of Eric Clapton, but I like his music and care precisely as much about his life as he does about mine.) And so on.

But when I open my presents, it's the same stuff in reverse, though I guess I'm nowhere near as good at it as is the missus. I do my level best to look excited at receiving Simon Jenkins' book of *100 Great Churches*, but really I know that it's going on the coffee table for about a month and then on the bookshelves for the rest of my life.

But the worst thing, really, the very worst thing about being a Grumpy Old Man at Christmas is that this is the time when everyone thinks it's fun to have a laugh at your grumpiness. So they buy you a hat with 'Under-gardener' written on it, which I personally find so amusing that I'm in serious danger that my sides will split. You receive greetings cards with what someone obviously thinks is a joke on the front about some flatulent old scrooge at Christmas. You receive a bottle of wine with 'Old Git' written on it, and then you've got to put on that long-suffering Grumpy Old Man expression and pretend to be taking it all in good part while everyone else takes the piss out of you.

Had your fun everyone? Oh good, now leave me alone so I can watch *The Guns of Navarone* on the telly.

I'm not going to go on about all the other things that Grumpy Old Men find irritating at Christmas because life is too short and so is this book. Suffice to say that it includes awful Christmas telly, being nice to neighbours and relatives you don't like, eating and drinking too much, putting up the decorations, taking down the decorations, and all that dreadful false bonhomie and 'goodwill to all men'. Rory McGrath had it right at the end of the programme we made about Christmas: when it's all over and people ask, 'How was your Christmas?' you never ever hear anyone say, 'It was fantastic. I had the best Christmas ever. It was wonderful.' What people say is, 'Yeah, it was all right. Quiet. Yes, quiet family Christmas. Quiet.' And you say, 'Yes, mine was crap as well.'

Birthdays aren't a lot better, and the best thing that can be said about them is that they come and go a lot more swiftly than Christmas. No months and months of build-up, and no turkey fricassée for days on end afterwards. Of course, the best thing about birthdays if you are a grumpy old bastard is that they are all about receiving presents and good wishes, and not about having to give any in return. They are the oral sex of annual festivities. But even they get on your nerves eventually. At what stage in your life does the downside of 'another year older' outweigh the upside of 'everyone gets to make a fuss of me and I get to behave like an even bigger brat than usual all day'? 35? 38? 45? Certainly, once you are over 40 it really does seem to be open season for everyone to start seriously having a laugh at your expense.

Oh, how absolutely hilarious, a bottle of Sanatogen. Oh, how droll, a subscription to *Saga* magazine. How wonderfully original, one of those little heated foot spas. (As a matter of fact I've always thought I might like one of those, but have never actually been given one.)

'We're not laughing at you,' my wife will console. 'We're laughing with you.'

'How can that be?' I respond. 'I'm not bloody laughing.' Yes, that's right, I have a mental age of 12.

Speaking of which, do you sometimes forget how old you are? I do. I think I'm so allergic to the idea of pretending to be younger than I am that I mentally start embracing the next year three or four months before my birthday. So that by the time the birthday actually comes around, I'm used to the idea of being 52, so I think I must be 53. Does that happen to you? No? Maybe I shouldn't have mentioned it.

Mother's Day and Father's Day are a bloody triumph for the marketing people, aren't they? How cool was it to think that one up? If you are a card manufacturer or retailer, or a florist, or confectioner, Mother's Day must be just another version of Christmas – cunningly placed sufficiently far enough away in the calendar from Christmas to give your profit-and-loss account a good boost.

Father's Day, not quite so easy, but an opportunity for all those people who produce totally useless gadgets that could only ever be an impulse buy. An electric cigar cutter. A device to imprint your initials on your golf balls. A 'Galileo's Thermometer', which seems to be a glass tube filled with water and gel-filled spheres that go up and down, or a clock that works with moving ball-bearings. More and more ingenious and less and less practical ways of getting a cork out of a wine bottle. And the funny thing is that you are quite touched anyone has bothered, and for a day you fiddle with your new toy while you're thinking, and after a while it becomes part of the clutter on your desk, and begins its long journey from your desk drawer, eventually to a cupboard, thence to a cardboard box in the loft, and finally, maybe 15 years later, to the charity shop or dump. Now is that grumpy? I'll say.

I've left the best till last. The apogee of exploitation and manipulation. No, it's not St Patrick's Day or Burns Night, nothing so mundane. It's Valentine's Day, 14 February. International day of ripping off young lovers. Congratulations, guys, this one takes the proverbial heart-shaped biscuit.

So the first thing to know about Valentine's Day is that you cannot simply ignore it. Not an option. Don't even consider it. You might even agree between you, 'Let's not buy any cards or presents this year, it's all so silly,' but take my advice. Don't fall for it. If you do, you can be as sure as night follows day that by the morning of the 14th you'll regret it and will feel like shit. Buy a card. Buy some flowers. Do something special. Or one of these at the very least.

Whatever you do, you know that you're going to be royally ripped off – and it's getting worse every year. This year my daughter and her boyfriend started planning arrangements for Valentine's Day weeks in advance. (God knows where we went wrong with her upbringing.) Every restaurant they called indicated a minimum charge – sometimes of £60 or £70. Some of them would only take bookings at 7 p.m. or 9.30 p.m. so that they could use every table at least twice in the evening. Every nightclub they called had inflated its already extortionate entrance fees. Red roses, get this, were retailing at twice the price you would have paid a week earlier or a week later.

And why do we allow ourselves to fall for it? Because we're all idiots, that's why. Without the independence of mind or balls to say, 'Up yours, I'm not going to be mugged. Go piss up a rope.'

So, special occasions? A wonderful time for all the rest of you to have a grumpy around. Don't let us spoil your enjoyment: just pop us in a corner and allow us to mumble 'Humbug' or 'Bollocks' or whatever is the appropriate festive greeting for the particular occasion. That'll keep you happy, and that'll make us happy too.

CHAPTER 6

What does this mean for our loved ones?

First of all, it needs to be said that it is a terrible mistake to invite your partner to think about how she copes with living with you. Chances are that she has just become acclimatised to your little idiosyncrasies and foibles over the last years, and hasn't really given a lot of conscious thought to what a pain in the neck you are. If you find yourself writing a book about being a Grumpy Old Man and therefore need some perspective on grumpies from someone who has to exist in close proximity, there is an inevitable risk that they're going to start thinking along the lines of, 'Yeah, why the hell do I have to put up with that?' And then you're in trouble.

In my case, my wife has worked out a *modus operandi* for dealing with me over years. When I asked her to think about it for this book, I have to admit that I was surprised that she didn't have to think too hard. It turns out that she has become pretty used to coping with a whole range of behavioural abnormalities, and has a range of well-tried and tested techniques and procedures.

For example, from time to time over the years I have heard anecdotes from her about conversations and events that have occurred when all her friends and their husbands are having dinner together or are at parties. If I'm honest, it may have occurred to me now and then that it was sort of odd that we had not been not invited to the event in question. However, it has always been such a source of such relief to me that we haven't had to go to these dinners and parties that I've resisted any temptation I might have had to ask.

Anyway, upon enquiry for the purposes of this chapter, it turns out that my wife has simply explained to her various friends that she is married to a grumpy old git, who doesn't really like going out and socialising, and that therefore she is much better off simply seeing them on her own at lunchtime.

Now I have to confess that I have distinctly mixed feelings when I hear this. First among them is an immense sense of gratitude towards my wife, who I know would secretly like to be among the couples who spend the summer hobnobbing at one family barbecue after another, but has decided to spare me from what she knows would be for me a form of medieval torture. Can you imagine it? All that standing next to some plonker in a hat and apron and discussing the merits of his super-duper new gas-powered outside grill with the built-in stay-hot tray?

On the other hand, I also get a slight wave of nausea that feels suspiciously like guilt. Whereas all her friends obviously look forward to these occasions and download all the gossip afterwards, it appears that I make myself such a liability for her that, rather than drag me along knowing that I'll be miserable and grumpy for days before and afterwards, she would rather not go at all.

This also explains what, until now, I had always thought was the odd way that many of my wife's friends treat me on the rare occasions that I meet them. Sort of slightly wary. Like maybe they don't know how I'm going to respond. A bit like approaching the glass between you and the orang-utan at the zoo. You want to see him move, but you're afraid to provoke him too much in case you get a sudden outburst and scare the living daylights out of yourself.

I understood this better when I learnt that, when talking about me to her friends, my wife refers to me as 'Darth'.

And I realise that in my wife's friends' households, from time to time, the subject must have come up about why we hadn't apparently been invited to this summer party or that dinner party, and the woman will have explained to her husband, 'Oh, she's nice enough, but unfortunately she's married to a grumpy old bastard.' Their husbands have probably responded with 'Poor woman,' but my theory is that they have then secretly envied me for having been saved from going through all the time-wasting bollocks. Or maybe that's only in my imagination.

Just now and again, maybe once a year in the summer, either I'll weaken or she'll weaken, or maybe it's one of the three couples I actually quite like, and we'll agree to accept an invitation. It seems like a good idea at the time, but as the day approaches, I always get less enthusiastic. By the time the event actually comes around, I'm reminding her why it is that she always fends off these invitations.

'Are these trousers all right?'

'No, too casual.'

'I thought it was a barbecue.'

'It is, but sawn-off 20-year-old Levis aren't "casual"… they make you look like a prat.'

In my heart I know she's right, and if she'd said it was OK to wear them, I'd have had my own misgivings. However, this exchange has given me the excuse I need to behave like a schoolboy.

'What about these then?'

'They're your work trousers.'

'I know but at least they're a bit smarter.'

'They look like you're going to the office.'

'OK,' so now at this point I am totally unreasonable, 'what the hell do I have to wear to fit in with your cookie-cutter friends and their cookie-cutter husbands?'

'What about those nice light trousers I bought you from Marks & Spencer?'

There you are – we're back to sodding Blue Harbour again!

Inevitably it will be a red-hot day and we'll set off in the car. She asks me if I plan to be difficult all afternoon, and I feel a genuine sense of grievance. I thought I was being perfectly affable. She agrees, but apparently I've been exuding that 'I'm not sure what we're doing here' demeanour without actually knowing I'm doing it.

Now I have to admit that I am being a bit of a bastard here. Though in truth, nothing unreasonable is being asked of me, I am giving out subtle messages of being a bit of a martyr.

'No, you go off and have a good chat to Margery and Annie. Don't worry at all about me. I'll have a lovely time chatting to Dave about his new promotion to deputy-executive vice-president of time-keeping and I can talk to Bob about the new codes on actuarial tables being adopted by the life-insurance industry.'

'Do you want to turn the car round?'

Now I should point out at this stage that we're in the car together and I'm driving. Although my wife is an excellent driver and has driven tens of thousands of miles safely over 20 years, she will never drive when I am in the car. Why is this? Because when I am in the car she is a shit driver. And why is this? Well, of course it's all my fault.

Whereas normally she is changing the gears smoothly, doing effortless hill-starts, coping with traffic in the London rush hour, with me sitting beside her she's changing gear in the wrong direction, too soon or too late, waiting for hours with a clear road at a junction and then setting off when a juggernaut is nearly upon us, and heading off with the hand-brake on.

'Is there a problem?' I might enquire.

'It's you.'

'What did I say?'

'You don't have to say anything. I just know you're being critical.'

Now whereas I am prepared to accept all the blame for about 99 per cent of such exchanges, in this case I'm genuinely at a loss. I was going to say that I positively make an effort to be relaxed while in the passenger seat of my wife's car, but I realise that 'making an effort to be relaxed' is perfectly possible to send out the sort of signals she's talking about.

But what's a guy to do? I never comment when the Belgian driving the juggernaut has to screech to a halt and misses us by the width of hand-made chocolate. I don't wince when the clutch going down and the change of gear are out of sync by two seconds, and I don't look round to see if we have left the gear-box a smouldering pile of metal in the road behind us. I don't push my foot down on an imaginary brake when we're hurtling towards a pedestrian crossing and three nuns are obviously about to cross the road. But am I exuding a bit of tension? Oh, all right, yes, I probably am.

But this is circular. I'm tense because she's driving like it's her first day on the road: she's driving like she's auditioning to be one of the idiots in the TV series *Driving School*, and it's all because I'm tense. I have to say that we've managed to find a way around most of the little irritations involved in living with the same person for a long time, but we haven't worked out how to crack that one.

So anyway, how is she coping? Well, I asked her to make a few notes, and was a bit mortified when I read them. There's me, all these years, thinking how easy-going I am and what a relative pleasure it must be to live with me, when all the time it turns out to be the equivalent of becoming accustomed to living with a serious physical deformity: you get used to it in the end but you never actually forget you've got the handicap.

I think it also needs to be said before we go into further detail that by and large Grumpy Old Men seem to end up with far nicer wives than they deserve. This seems to be a common theme among most of the self-confessed grumpies I met while we were making the programmes. Jeremy Clarkson told us how nowadays he has a rule that whenever someone new goes into the family address book, someone else has to come out. Apparently, they must be so popular that he just can't cope with any more friends. When I heard this, I immediately sensed a kindred spirit, and was honestly amazed that the same thought hadn't occurred to me. That was probably because I never look in our address book because I never want to contact anyone in it, so I wouldn't know who's in and who's out. However, Jeremy confessed that he was frequently thwarted in this thoroughly sensible measure because his wife, unlike him, is basically a nice person.

Grumpies among my personal acquaintances all have nicer wives then they are entitled to expect – in some cases much nicer – and I suspect that this is not a coincidence. It's not that nice women are attracted to grumpy men – if that were so, I'd be the most desirable man in the neighbourhood. And I'm not. I've no idea who is because I don't know anyone in the neighbourhood. I just know it's not me. Anyway, my theory is that our partners become so embarrassed at our anti-social and generally bloody contrary behaviour that they do whatever they can to compensate.

They also, I suspect, have a particular talent for sensing when to confront and when to go into 'Yes, dear' mode. As years go by, no doubt everyone mellows a bit, and the

'Yes, dear' option becomes more frequently adopted. These days I find I'm getting 'Yes, deared' quite a lot. 'Can anyone tell me why we have to sit through the full opening credits of three different Hollywood film producers before we get to the single caption "Lilliput Films in association with Columbia Pictures with a Tristar presentation"? That's another minute and a half gone.'

'Yes, dear.'

'Have you noticed how there are fewer and fewer beans and more and more of that horrible tomato sauce in the baked bean tin?'

'Yes, dear.'

'Why is it, do you suppose, that if we check in for the plane first, last or somewhere in the middle, our suitcase is always the very last one to come off the conveyer belt?'

'Yes, dear.'

She says I was always a bit like this. It seems I've always tended to be a bit intolerant. Always been argumentative. And always had a nasty habit of stating something as though I know it to be a fact, even when I don't actually have the slightest idea what I'm talking about. And the more I'm challenged on it, the more adamant I get.

However, it seems that I have also got worse in recent years. Which more or less acquits the whole thesis of this book. Whereas I used to confine myself to the odd remark when someone said something terminally stupid on the television, I now provide a more or less continuous running commentary on John Stapleton's stripy jacket, or Michael Howard's appalling smugness, or Carol Vorderman's over-dramatic cheekbones.

While, apparently, I sometimes used to drive a whole journey listening in silence to the radio, now it seems I can't drive to Safeway without commenting on the new traffic island or the closure of the Robin Hood gate into Richmond Park or the fact that this road has been in a constant state of cable-laying for five months.

And while sometimes I'd eat a sandwich and say how nice it was and thank her for making it, I'm now apparently dropping odd bits of tomato or egg down the best pullover I shouldn't really be wearing, and swearing and cursing, with the implication that it's my wife's fault.

However, for some reason best known to herself, she seems willing, so far, to put up with it: and, indeed, she did produce a range of tips for dealing with my repertoire of unpleasant personal habits, which I'm certainly not going to share in this volume. Self-flagellation can be taken too far.

I will share one of them, though, because fellow grumpies might find it provides a clue to one of life's mysteries: what has happened to that T-shirt I so loved and haven't seen for a while? This is about how she deals with my alleged tendency to hang on to old items of clothing for far longer than is sensible, or possibly hygienic. She reminds me of a particular pair of green trainers that I bought from Marks & Spencer in their pre-Blue Harbour days – in about 1980 to be precise. I was still wearing these jogging trainers regularly in 2002, and began to get a bit grumpy that some of the lining was coming out. It seems, and I must admit that I had forgotten this, that I seriously toyed with

the idea of taking them back to the shop to complain that they were coming apart. She claims that I hoped they would be so impressed by my brass neck that they would spring me a new pair on the house. Seems a good idea to me: I've no idea why I didn't do it.

Anyhow, I now learn that her technique is to take these items of clothing away for washing on a regular basis, but to extend the intervals before they are re-produced washed and ironed. Then one day they go in the back of a drawer in the hope that I'll forget about them, and eventually, if not explicitly missed, they can be thrown out.

Now this has come as quite a revelation to me – not least that my wife can be this devious – and certainly I'll be exploring the deep recesses of my various cupboards and drawers for that favourite T-shirt with Frank Zappa on the front, which I came by second-hand in 1976 and which, come to think of it, I haven't seen for a while.

It also seems to be a good idea for the partner of a grumpy to cast a quick eye over him before he leaves the house. It's been known for me to go out wearing old clogs, a 27-year-old T-shirt, sawn-off jeans and carrying a cup of tea.

However, the key tip, the one golden rule apparently, is that she also strongly recommends giving your pet grumpy as much personal space as you can – especially space with a heavy door in between her and him. A particular room dedicated to his boy's toys, and stuff, is favourite; failing that, some space in the attic, or, of course, a shed. Grumpies need a space to seethe in.

It seems that, if properly looked after and kept clean and well fed, you can get many years of pleasure out of your own grumpy. I'm not at all sure I know what I think about that, but hey, what's a grump to do?

CHAPTER 7

Where does that leave us?

Well, what now? You might well ask. When I review what I've written over the last 200 pages or so, I'm appalled. They describe a life, don't they, that's a very long way from the one that was promised to those poor little sods sitting in their monochromatic schoolrooms, with scratchy 16mm film flapping through noisy projectors depicting the world of the future.

There's not a lot of whooshing about in steel and glass capsules hovering over monorails, is there? Not a lot of clear-skinned, bright-eyed, well-adjusted work colleagues gliding around wearing skin-tight jumpsuits. Not a lot of 'electricity too cheap to meter' or robots making the breakfast. Not a lot of integration, rehabilitation, reconciliation or, indeed, anything else good ending in 'ation'.

It's coming up to 2005 and we still can't control the weather, or disease, or racism, or poverty, or crime, or pollution, or greed, or intolerance. For the life of us, we can't even control bloody public bloody transport.

No, it didn't turn out the way we were promised it would when we were in school. It also didn't turn out the way we believed it would in the summer of love. We stood at the dawning of the Age of Aquarius and sang, 'Let the sun shine in'. We really did think that 'What we need is a great big melting pot'. Heaven knows, we even thought that 'In the end, the love you take is equal to the love you make'. Of course, it was twaddle, but we didn't know that then.

But instead of taking Arlo Guthrie's advice to 'walk into the draft office, wherever we happen to be, sing a bar of "Alice's Restaurant", and walk out', we stood by and ate our fish fingers as the living shit was bombed out of the people of former Yugoslavia. Instead of taking Marc Bolan's advice to 'Ride a White Swan', we allowed cows to eat their own brains, thereby giving rise to CJD. Instead of listening to Hurricane Smith when he pleaded with us that we 'Don't Let It Die', we hunted hundreds of animal species to extinction and poured so much nuclear waste into the North Sea that the fish have two heads.

None of that let the sun shine in. We didn't give peace a chance. And to add insult to injury, we didn't even have the decency to die before we got old. So now we're getting ready to be a huge and wearisome burden on our children and grandchildren because, as Will Self so vividly put it, we're all living far too long. 'There's going to be thousands of us wearing denim and listening to dreadful music on sort of – not on Walkmans – on Zimmermans – you know, like Bob Dylan – Zimmerman. Brilliant, I've coined it.' A vivid and lurid image indeed.

But, that all said, the funny thing is that all the bollocks that replaced it didn't work either, did it? The politics that ungraciously shoved all our old nonsense to one side hasn't delivered any better. Oh sure, we're all a lot better off materially than we once were, even grumpy old sods can see that. Most people in the UK are better off financially and most of us are healthier – apart from the obesity, that is. There are fewer of us doing filthy and dangerous manual jobs. Most of the poor seem to have about the same number of possessions – house, car, colour TV, video – as the well-to-do had when we were kids. If you'd told our ancestors 200 years ago that the poorest people in society would also be the fattest, they would have been unable to work out how. Crime isn't actually rising, even though fear of crime is. Most of our biggest rivers, which were open sewers when we were kids, now have fish in them.

So why is it, do you suppose, that it's all so much better, but it all feels so much worse? Despite the undoubted material improvements, surveys designed to find out how happy we are find no improvement over the last 50 years; and that's not just Grumpy Old Men, that's the general population. Today one-third of visits to the GP are in some way linked to depression, and a quarter of us will receive treatment for clinical depression at some time in our lives.

Wow! How scary is that?

Maybe it's part of the human condition; we're not programmed by evolution to be content because if we were, we would stagnate. But it's also possible that there is something else going on here.

We all know that the economics of the society we live in today require us to believe that the acquisition and consumption of material things will make us happier. Thus we are bombarded from every direction with stuff that, they tell us, will make our lives complete. The idea is that we should all strive hard to acquire whatever is the particular object of desire of the moment – the bottle of Coke, or the iPod, or a new Mini Cooper – and that will make us happy.

So of course we have striven for those things, and very often we've acquired them. But, it turns out, this hasn't made us happy either. Getting a new designer watch or T-shirt or pair of shoes or cool mobile might give some of us a lift for a minute or an hour, or in some cases maybe as much as a day, but it doesn't actually make us any nearer to being content. Buying a new car might make us feel good for a week or so, but overall people with a brand new Mercedes don't report themselves as more fulfilled than people with an ageing VW Polo.

So while it didn't turn out to be true that 'All you need is love', it also hasn't turned out that all you need is money or material possessions either. Which may be why everyone from Madonna to Tom Cruise, from Beyoncé to bloody stupid Sting is now desperately seeking something else. What to do when you get what you thought you wanted and find out that it isn't?

Cosmopolitan, the magazine that promised women 'now you can have it all', recently appointed a 'spirituality editor' because now that they've 'got it all', they've found that there is still something missing. And no one knows what it is.

They are looking for answers in everything from Buddhism to tantric sex. Everything from ayurvedic yoga to the Atkins diet. Good luck to them.

As for us grumpies, we've held the reins of power, are about to hand them over to the next generation, and we know we didn't cut it.

Could we have stopped hunger in Africa if we had really set our minds to it? Of course we could.

Could we have addressed the worldwide AIDS epidemic if we had made it an international number-one priority? Of course we could.

Could we have decided not to drop a lot of bombs on people from other religions, and instead sat down and asked them, 'What is it with you guys?' Of course we could.

But we didn't. And now it's too late. We're passing these problems on to our children, who don't look remotely more ready or equipped to deal with them sensibly than we were.

Between them and us we're just going to elect another set of pompous halfwits to replace the current set of pompous halfwits, and we're all going to sit back and watch the world go to hell.

Are we angry? No, we were angry when we were students and into our 20s. It takes more energy than we've got to be angry. That's all behind us.

Are we acquiescent? No, we're not quite ready for that yet. That's coming soon, I hope. And my wife hopes so too.

Just at the moment what we simply are is grumpy. There is nothing to be done for or about us, and you've got a choice of introducing voluntary euthanasia or putting up with us, boring and grumbling and whingeing into our alcohol-free beer, until eventually we shuffle off into our final dotage.

'I take it all back,' said Arthur Smith, and since we gave him the first words, we may as well give him the last. 'Everything I've said is rubbish. What really gets on my nerves is Grumpy Old Men moaning on about everything around them. Just shut up and get ready for the coffin.'

Hear, hear.

I'm outta here!

Acknowledgements

First of all I need to thank our cast of Grumpy Old Men, without whom none of this would be possible: Stephen Bayley, John Bird, Bill Bryson, Jeremy Clarkson, Felix Dexter, Bob Geldof, A. A. Gill, Michael Grade, Tony Hawks, Simon Hoggart, Neil Kinnock, Steve Jones, Richard Madeley, Andrew Marr, Rory McGrath, Bill Nighy, John O'Farrell, Matthew Parris, John Peel, John Sergeant, Will Self, John Sessions, Lemm Sissay, Arthur Smith, Rick Stein, Ken Stott, Antony Worrall Thompson, Rick Wakeman and Nigel Williams. It was a labour of love for them – it had to be because we paid them next to nothing. Then there is all the production team on the two series, notably Jackie Baker, Marina Fonseca, John Warwick, Tim White, Howard and Jeff the film editors, the incomparable Judy Lewis, and Geoffrey Palmer for the voiceover. Obviously Alan Lewens; he's the man. I want to thank Tom Archer, Jo Clinton-Davis and Maxine Watson at the BBC for allowing and, indeed, even encouraging us to be very silly, and Jane Root's husband for being sufficiently grumpy to enable her to recognise the phenomenon. Thanks also to Ben Dunn at BBC Books (far too young to be grumpy, but exhibiting worrying signs), Rachel Copus and Shirley Patton. I want to acknowledge my various mates who contributed, consciously or unconsciously, to the ideas in this book, especially Andrew McLaughlin and Peter Hayton. And I want to apologise unreservedly to our friends, who've been totally and unfairly misrepresented throughout. My daughter Alex, poor kid, has had to put up with it all her life, but I guess she hasn't had a lot of choice. Greatest thanks therefore go to my wife Marilyn, who had a choice and still stuck with it. Is that heroic or what?

ALSO AVAILABLE FOR
GRUMPY OLD MEN EVERYWHERE;

Arthur Smith reads
The Official Grumpy Old Men Handbook

Available from 20th September 2004
priced £12.99

Warning: This CD could cause road rage!

Crap Cars

Richard Porter

0 563 52210 0

From the Austin Allegro to the Renault Safrane, and from the MGB to the Volkswagen Beetle, this book brings together 50 of the worst cars ever to grace the roads of Britain.

The book features everything from the aesthetically pathetic to the mechanically misguided and includes tales of the most bizarre and appalling cock-ups in motoring history.

With full-colour photos to illustrate each entry, this chronicle of classically Crap Cars will transport you back to the beige and brown world of the seventies and eighties and your very own Morris Marina.

The Authorised Biography of Ronnie Barker

Bob McCabe

0 563 52211 9

Ronnie Barker is one of the best-loved and most celebrated entertainers in British television history. As well as starring in the ever popular and critically acclaimed sitcoms *Porridge* and *Open All Hours*, he was, of course, one of the bespectacled Two Ronnies, who topped the TV Charts for more than 15 years and are returning to our screens in spring 2005.

A celebration of Ronnie's life and career, published to coincide with Ronnie's 75th birthday, this book contains original contributions from people who have worked with and know him best including John Cleese, David Jason (who provides the foreword), David Frost, Eric Idle, and Michael Palin.

Written with the full consent and collaboration of Ronnie himself, this biography is full of interviews and unseen personal illustrations from his own collection.

Bob McCabe is a respected author and journalist and contributes regularly to film magazines and BBC radio arts programmes. He is the author of several books.

Eric Morecambe: Life's not Hollywood, it's Cricklewood

Gary Morecambe

0 563 52186 4

In this fascinating biography, Eric's son, Gary Morecambe, describes what it's like to grow up in the presence of one of the best-loved and most fondly remembered of all British comedy greats.

Eric and Ernie brought sunshine and laughter to the people of Britain for an amazing 22 years. This highly personal biography includes photos from the Morecambe family archive and unseen extracts from his father's personal diaries.

Frank and outspoken, this book provides a compelling insight into the man behind the laughter, a man who was constantly worried that one day he would be 'found out', who never lost his love of Long John Silver impressions, and who continued to work until his death from heart disease at only 58 years of age.

The League of Gentlemen: Scripts and That

0 563 48775 5

The League of Gentlemen were first noticed at Edinburgh in 1996 and scooped the prestigious Perrier Award the following year. Their first BBC show was Radio 4's 'On The Town With The League Of Gentlemen' and was followed swiftly by a ground-breaking BBC2 series, which unleashed the freakish inhabitants of Royston Vasey on the British public. Two further series followed, as well as a one-hour Christmas special, and enjoyed a devoted following.

Here, for the first time, the scripts are presented in full in this vast volume. Beautifully illustrated with over 800 previously unseen pictures from the League's private collection together with early drawings by the writers, this book is a must-have for fans of the series. The book also includes early drafts of the scripts, private letters and memos, and a full character list detailing every one of the bizarre characters who populate Royston Vasey.

You Have Been Watching ... The Autobiography of David Croft

0 563 48739 9

As the writer and creator of some of the best loved series in British TV history, David Croft has captivated audiences with such timelessly lovable sitcoms as *Dad's Army*, *Hi de Hi*, *'Allo 'Allo* and *Are You Being Served?*

David's autobiography reflects on a life that has revolved around showbusiness – his mother was the famous actress Annie Croft – and provides a privileged insight into the workings of British TV in what Croft suggests was the golden era of the '60s to '80s. The book also illuminates Croft himself as he tells of his experiences during the war years and the ups and downs of his family life.

Characteristically warm and funny, David Croft's autobiography is a first-class account of a life surrounded by celebrity. Devotees of his programmes will enjoy a wealth of anecdotes about actors such as Clive Dunn and Wendy Richards and relish the behind-the-scenes insights into the personalities and working styles of some of Britain's most famous television actors.

The Office
The Scripts: Volume 1

0 563 48847 6

The Office
The Scripts: Volume 2

0 563 48741 0

Do you know what upsets David Brent?

Wasted talent, yeah? People could come to him, and they could go, "'scuse me David, but you've been in the business 12 years, can you just spare us a moment to tell us how to, you know, run a team, how to keep them task-orientated while, you know, happy?"

But they don't.

That's the tragedy.

So the Brentmeister General is now prepared to share with us the scenes of his daily life: the scenarios that really illustrate the principles of great team management; his morale-boosting comedy (remember when he got Dawn to actually believe she was sacked?); his fund of earthy wisdom ('there should be no ego when you're pulling together to do something good…'); along with glimpses of the fervent soul beyond the work-related arena, the impassioned singer-songwriter of the potentially highly successful band Foregone Conclusion (a.k.a. supported by Texas).

These scripts will show how anyone can be a great boss and a funny person, how to use humour to boost morale, how to have a laugh at work, with women, at us. Investment in people. That's what it's all about really. The staff. Letting them know that they are our most important commodity. It's like, if you're cleaning a floor, and you're up against it, then come to me, and I'll help us clean our floor together…not literally.

Each volume includes 500 screengrabs from each series, together with such treasures as unseen email correspondence between David Brent and his BBC Producer.

The Office: The Scripts volumes 1 and *2* are definitive comedy script books, providing fans with an invaluable opportunity to relive their favourite moments over and over again.

'Original and accurate and painfully funny: it will have every office in the country twitching with spasms of recognition… This is a gem.' – *The Times*

Terry Wogan

Is it me?

0 563 53422 2

Terry Wogan is one of Britain's best-loved radio and television celebrities – witty, charming and relaxed, he has undoubtedly captured the nation's heart. Here, for the first time ever, Terry tells his life story from his beginnings as a young Limerick boy to his incredible success as an enduring celebrity of shows such as *Wogan* and *The Eurovision Song Contest*.

Is It Me? is written in Terry's own inimitable style, with self-deprecating humour and a wry take on everyday life. The story is a delightfully observed, light-hearted journey through Terry's personal and professional lives that will delight his millions of fans.

After reluctantly starting his career in banking, Terry escaped to make a sucessful break into broadcasting with RTE. Fronting *Children in Need*, *Wogan* and *The Eurovision Song Contest* and collecting millions of listeners to his morning BBC 2 radio show, *Wake Up To Wogan*, he is now the most prolific and popular presenter at the BBC.

'I am sure it's a challenging read' Sir David Frost

'I don't remember him' Jimmy Young